D0917400

DISCARD

SANDS OF TIME

A Century of Racing in Daytona Beach

WILLIAM P. LAZARUS

WITH ADDITIONAL MATERIAL BY
J. J. O'MALLEY

www.SportsPublishingLLC.com

ACKNOWLEDGMENTS

No author succeeds alone. I am grateful to everyone involved with this special project: my parents, my wife and daughter, who always thought, someday, at least one of the many books I have written would be published; friends like Cynthia Schuster-Eakin, Mike Silverstein, Miriam Huske and Jon Swebilius, who always encouraged me; colleagues like J.J. O'Malley, senior editor at ISC Publications who supplied information on the early motorcycle races and his own expertise to the text; Cindy Dusenbury, Editorial supervisor, who edited my drafts in her usual fine manner; Tom Pokorny, ISC Publications president, who, when he hired me, told me he wanted this book written; Buz McKim, then-ISC Archivist who was unstinting in his help; Skip Clayton, a fellow sportswriter who suggested contacting Sports Publishing; and Lynnette Bogard at Sports Publishing who oversaw the production of this book.

ISBN: 1-58261-784-8

Director of production: Susan M. Moyer
Coordinating editor: Lynnette Bogard
Book design, senior project manager: Jennifer L. Polson
Cover design: Joseph Brumleve
Photo imaging: Kerri Baker and Christine Mohrbacher

Visit us on the Internet at www.sportspublishingllc.com

Daytona International Speedway has three "grooves," or lanes that drivers can use to circle the track. The inside line is typically the shortest and fastest way to get to Victory Lane. Motorsports Images & Archives Photo

Fans lined the finish line to watch Malcolm Campbell complete a record run in 1933. He averaged 272.108 mph that year, topping his old record, set the year before, by about 17 mph. Motorsports Images & Archives Photo

CONTENTS

FOREWORD BY BILL FRANCE

The story of racing in Daytona Beach is really the story of my dad and my family. "Big Bill" France moved here in the early 1930s with my mother and me. He was attracted to this community by the racing on the beach. For decades, drivers had come here to test their courage and skill, setting land-speed records on that hard sand.

In 1935, he joined hundreds of people on the beach to watch Sir Malcolm Campbell set the land-speed record at around 278 mph.

My dad helped set up and promote the first stock car race in 1936 with a friend of his, Sig Haugdahl, a former speed racer. They had to struggle the first couple of years, but soon, racing along the shores of the Atlantic Ocean became very popular.

Then, after the war, Dad realized that there had to be an organization to run stock car racing and make it a legitimate sport. So, he called a meeting in Daytona Beach in 1947 and set up the National Association for Stock Car Auto Racing (NASCAR). He also recognized there wasn't enough room for all the new people coming to Daytona Beach to enjoy the beach and the weather and for race cars. So, he built Daytona International Speedway in 1959. I helped do some of the work of that now-legendary track, which is home to the Daytona 500.

Today, stock car racing is rapidly gaining on football as the most popular sport in this country.

NASCAR annually sanctions races all over the United States, from events on small, neighborhood tracks right up to races that draw as many as 230,000 people and millions more on television.

Daytona Beach sits in the heart of all that growth, the home of racing for more than 100 years.

This is the story of how one small community became the center of a major sport. It starts with a simple promotion for a hotel and a few wealthy owners showing off their cars. A century later, this little community, my home for more than 70 years, remains the byword for speed, courage and skill.

It's been quite a ride. Strap yourself in and enjoy it.

Bill France
Vice Chairman, NASCAR

Bucky Sager (No. 101) and Ed Rooney (No. 73) battle for position coming through the South Turn of the Beach-Road Course in 1951. Sager, driving a 1949 Plymouth, won this tussle. He finished 25th; Rooney, in a 1947 Ford, ended up 37th. Motorsports Images & Archives Photo

INTRODUCTION

Here and there, like leaves torn from a book and sprinkled by the wind, images of Daytona Beach's century-old race history infuse the area's landscape. Some are well disguised in street signs, maybe a plaque or a monument. Others stand as obvious as the Roman Coliseum. Some were never more than a gleam in the planner's eye, dying in committee or forgotten at funding time. All are evidence why Daytona Beach is known as "The World Center of Racing."

At the core is perhaps the most famous race track in the world—Daytona International Speedway. Hundreds of thousands of race fans flood local streets for NASCAR's Daytona 500 in February and the Pepsi 400 in July. They come, too, for the legendary endurance road race, the Rolex 24 at Daytona, motorcycle centerpieces like the Daytona 200 and various historic race-car events.

DAYTONA USA, the Volusia Speedway Park, other local race tracks and various go-kart sites attest to racing's place through the county.

Amid the modern structures today, the true beginnings of motorsports still linger. The real history of racing in Daytona Beach cannot be fully appreciated without understanding how deeply racing is woven into the fiber of life here. From the Speedway north to Ormond Beach, east to the wide sands of Daytona, south to Ponce Inlet and west to DeLand, many sites reflect this area's intense motorsports' tradition.

Much of Daytona's race history has been disguised or has slipped away, bypassed in an endless battle against time. The original beach courses—the first in Ormond, the second spanning Ponce Inlet and Daytona Beach Shores—have vanished into the sea.

The Museum of Speed, which was opened in 1955 by NASCAR historian Bill Tuthill, closed in 1972. The Ridgewood Avenue museum was once the main repository for race history. NASCAR archivist Buz McKim can remember spending endless hours there learning about racing. Its contents became the basis of today's International Motorsports Hall of Fame in Talladega, Alabama.

The original Memorial Stadium, used for dirt-track races into the 1970s, became a Daytona Beach Community College parking lot. Another landmark, the Ormond Garage, was originally built by the railroad in 1904. The building was adapted in 1903 to service automobiles that competed on the hard-packed sands. It burned down in 1976, but a plaque commemorates the site at 113 E. Granada Blvd.

The existing Ormond Garage, 48 W. Granada Blvd., was built to service cars in 1919. Today, it houses period artifacts and photos from that bygone era.

Some markers have been erected, but they haven't always hung around. In the spring of 2000, the Daytona Beach Historic Preservation Board discovered as many as five markers honoring this area's history—including racing—had vanished. One of the plaques commemorated Sir Malcolm Campbell, the English insurance man who set several land-speed records on the "World's Most Famous Beach" before opting to try his luck on the salt flats in Utah.

A monument to the measured mile, the famed one-mile stretch of beach where some of the fastest cars in the world competed to set a land-speed record, has never come to fruition.

Travel back to Ormond Beach, the acknowledged "Birthplace of Speed," about 10 miles north of Daytona Beach. Its race heritage is recreated annually in a nostalgia-filled parade of antique cars. The city also hosts exhibition "races" on its hard-packed beach in November. One by one, reliving

A 1903 promotion to boost the Hotel Ormond led to the first races in Daytona Beach. Motorsports Images & Archives Photo

the past, cars from various eras line up to speed about a quarter-mile down the beach. There are no prizes, no trophies, simply the cheers of the hundreds of people who stand along the dunes to watch.

Early drivers did more than compete against each other. They wanted to set speed records. The flat, unusually hard beach seemed ideal, although drivers had to be careful not to be caught by the incoming tide or thrown off course by an occasional sandy bump.

To be sure the resulting speed was accurate, the lone national sanctioning body, the American Automobile Association, created a nine-mile course in the early 1900s. Four miles were used to build up speed: one mile for a run at full speed—dubbed the "Measured Mile"—and four miles to cool down. Cars drove north once, then duplicated the run heading south. The speeds generated during the two runs were then averaged to get the recognized time.

Whenever a driver scheduled an assault on the land-speed record, the Daytona Beach fire station, which still stands on the southeast corner of the intersection of Beach Street and Orange Avenue would set off its siren to alert spectators, police and the National Guard of the impending effort. Halifax Medical Center probably appreciated the notice, since drivers regularly crashed.

The track stretched from Ponce Inlet north to Daytona Beach. Daytona Beach Shores, incorporated in 1967 and encompassing about 1.1 square miles, contains the entire Measured Mile within its borders. It extended from Dunlawton Avenue to what is now the Oceans One condominium.

Now a small retirement community best known for its row of high-rise condominiums, officials in Daytona Beach Shores once drew up plans for a commemorative marker honoring the Measured Mile in the mid-1990s. The idea fizzled because of cost and the concern that any construction might bother endangered turtles.

Instead, the city constructed a carved monument to the late Otto Schultze, a former city councilman who had searched for Campbell's famous car, the Bluebird.

The monument features an image of the famed car, one of several identically named race cars that resemble the "Batmobile" of comic-book fame. The last-known version of the car, discovered rusting in a London junkyard in 1951 and eventually purchased by Bill France, now sits in DAYTONA USA, the motorsports-related attraction adjacent to the Daytona International Speedway.

Schultze's monument was dedicated in 1998 and is located in a small park a few yards north of the Daytona Beach Shores' City Hall complex. International Speedway Corporation, which owns race tracks around the country, donated the race flags that festoon the monument.

Surrounding the Schultze memorial are the Living Legends of Auto Racing Memorial Bricks, each engraved with the names of drivers, mechanics and other luminaries from racing's past. The bricks are purchased by anyone wanting to permanently honor someone in the racing community.

In the Daytona Beach Shores Community Center, a small display highlights a few of the drivers and equipment from the early years.

The nearby Daytona Hilton Oceanfront Resort contains the Oceanside Rotary Stock Car Hall of Fame on its first floor. Plaques on the wall recognize famed car drivers.

Less obvious is the Drive-in Christian Church. Once a drive-in movie theater, it was also the original registration site for drivers competing in the beach races from 1936 to 1958. It's located about a half mile south of Daytona Beach Shores City Hall on A1A.

To the north, along the historic Boardwalk in Daytona Beach, plaques recalling those early years of racing are posted adjacent to the Main Street Pier in a special exhibit. The renowned clocktower, long a symbol of Daytona Beach and located in the park behind the Adam's Mark Hotel, is named for Campbell.

Campbell also has his name attached to a Daytona Beach street and public school. The latter is located on Keech Street, so named in honor of driver Ray Keech. Another driver immortalized by a street sign is Major H.O.D. Segrave, an Englishman who was the first driver to wear a safety helmet. In 1927, Segrave set the land-speed record of 203.79 mph in his Sunbeam Mystery "S." Soon after, Daytona Beach started calling itself "The World's Most Famous Beach," a nod to its place in world race history.

Frank Lockhart, another speed racer, is also remembered by a street sign.

Although Campbell hit his peak in 1935 when he aimed at the bull's eye posted as a marker for the beginning of the Measured Mile and averaged 276.82 mph, concerns about safety on a beach at such speeds took him and the next Bluebird to Utah's salt flats.

However, a young mechanic watching Campbell's record run was drawn to racing. William H.G. France would eventually have a bigger impact on this community than the Englishman ever did. He also has a street named after him as does Richard Petty. The track was not forgotten. Anyone entering the city via State Route 92 is driving on International Speedway Boulevard.

Seeing the speed at which racers took their efforts to the West, city fathers discussed ways to keep crowds coming to Daytona Beach. Several proposals were made and rejected, but officials decided to build on the strong reputation the area had developed in motorsports. Having no track except the beach, the city moved south from the Ormond location and set up a 3.2-mile course from Dunlawton Avenue in Daytona Beach Shores to a spot across from where that community's City Hall now sits. It stretched about 1.6 miles north on the sand; and 1.6 miles south on A1A, the paved beachside thoroughfare that runs the length of the shoreline.

Today, in nearby Ponce Inlet, a restaurant located at 4511 S. Atlantic Ave. marks the northern end of the beach/road course—the famed "North Turn" for the younger of the two beach courses.

The first race was held there in 1936. Later, France, who served as the promoter, would shift the track further south to provide more room. He went on to help organize the National Association of Stock Car Auto Racing (NASCAR) in the late 1940s. NASCAR was to act as an umbrella organization for all stock-car races.

NASCAR set up its initial offices in the Selden Building, 800 Main Street, the sanctioning body used other locales around the city. As NASCAR grew, so did its use of area facilities. The old Armory, also on Ballough Road, was the site for the first pre-race inspections. Florida National Bank, then housed in a building that is now the home of the Halifax Historical Society on Beach Street downtown, handled finances for the new sanctioning body.

With the sport's continued success in Daytona Beach, racers moved into the area in order to be near the center of racing. Marshall Teague, who died in a 1959 crash, opened a gas station at the corner of Fairview and Ballough Road. Ray Fox, who still calls this area home, opened a garage at the foot of the Seabreeze Bridge.

The 42 South Peninsula site was NASCAR's headquarters until 1959. Daytona International Speedway opened that year and the offices moved there. NASCAR is now headquartered across the street from the Speedway in a former industrial complex, and entrance is gained from Bill France Boulevard.

In the last few years of his life, France maintained his private office in the Ballough Road site. The building once housed the International Speedway Corporation's archives. Archives has moved to the old Root Building on Fentress Boulevard, taking along France's office, which remains exactly as he left it, decorated with his personal photographs on the wall, various souvenirs and mementos.

These days, the main focus of racing is on the Daytona International Speedway. Yet, the hum of now-silent engines still lingers behind the roar of today's racing machines.

It's been that way for 100 years.

PROLOGUE

Wind regularly whips across the ocean's edge and drives round, white balls of foam across the shore in Daytona Beach like misplaced tumbleweeds. One of the frothy balls invariably takes the lead in this strange race, finally stopping beyond its companions. The competition is almost inevitable. Something about this flat, hard-packed beach cries out for speed.

People have been listening for 100 years. Throughout that time, Daytona has remained not only the site for incredible—sometimes even unbelievable—events on the track, but the heart of motorsports. Virtually every important driver in the past century has passed through here in the quest for glory. Alexander Winton, Ransom Olds and Henry Ford were the names in the beginning. They were followed by speed racers like Barney Oldfield, Bob Burman and Ralph DePalma, then Malcolm Campbell and Henry Segrave. Once stock cars were introduced, fans could enjoy the exploits of Bill France, Roy Hall and Bob "Cannonball" Baker. When NASCAR was created, it was led by hall of famers Lee Petty, Buck Baker, Ned Jarrett and Fred Lorenzen. They were succeeded in turn by Richard Petty, Cale Yarborough and David Pearson, then Darrell Waltrip, Dale Earnhardt, Ricky Rudd, Rusty Wallace, Mark Martin and Bill Elliott. Today, along with veterans Jeff Gordon, Bobby Labonte and Dale Jarrett, Dale Earnhardt Jr., Tony Stewart, Jimmie Johnson, Ryan Newman, Matt Kenseth and Jeff and Ward Burton are among the drivers propelling motorsports into the 21st century.

All of them have competed in Daytona and won renown because of their association with Daytona.

Almost every significant innovation in racing occurred here. Specialized engines debuted on the hard-packed beach. So did helmets, windshields and racing tires, timing devices, scoreboards and more.

The first large-scale auto races were held in Daytona when the rest of the country was still being introduced to the "horseless carriage." Records were scanty in the first decade of racing here and often incomplete. Accounts left by reports frequently disagree on even basic aspects of an event. All that's left are glimpses of faces, eyes staring straight ahead at the clear beach, hands firmly gripping steering wheels, and cars often little more than engines with wheels.

In time, the name Daytona became a synonym for speed. People know the definition. Today, the Daytona 500 draws in excess of 250,000 fans a year. The Pepsi 400 during the summer is the largest nighttime sporting event in the world. Speed Weeks alone contributes $561 million to the local economy, according to a 2002 report.

For more than 55 years, the center of the sport was the unusual, hard-packed beach. Today, racing resides in the legendary Daytona International Speedway. But, Daytona itself has remained a constant. This sun-splashed resort community along Florida's east coast continues to be the living embodiment of racing heritage.

That's why today's racers still test their courage not very far from where the foam balls roll along the beach and the sounds of 100 years of competition continually echo in the waves.

chapter one

FIRST YEARS

The wealth of racing history that permeates Daytona Beach masks its meager origins. At the turn of the 20th century, Daytona Beach was an isolated community located about 90 miles south of Jacksonville in east-central Florida. Few people had ever heard of it. No one thought racing would become its main industry. A long train ride was the best way to visit, although a boat might be found to carry an intrepid traveler. Cars were not much of an option 100 years ago. They only promised long, overland drives on shell-covered roads through mosquito-thick swamps. The long, hard beach was the ideal thoroughfare, although getting to it could require cutting through a palmetto forest or fording small streams.

Not many people were willing to hazard such a journey. Population estimates range from 4,000 to 6,000 people, picking up in the winter when a handful of cold Northerners straggled in to enjoy the warmer weather.

The few photographs from that era show unpaved, tree-lined streets, a few scattered homes, several stores and one large hotel situated a block from the Halifax River and less than a mile from the beach. That hotel became the key that would crank the engine of motorsports.

Bought in 1889 by financier Henry Flagler and expanded to cover 12 acres, the Hotel Ormond (later known as the Ormond Hotel) initially served as a luxury destination for wealthy tourists who took the Jacksonville, St. Augustine and Halifax River Railway along the east coast of Florida as far south as the Florida Keys. Flagler placed the hotel in Ormond Beach to spite Daytona Beach officials who declined to give in to his financial demands. Once the oldest wooden structure of its kind in the United States, the facility did not hold up well to time. Despite a spirited preservation effort by a handful of local residents, the hotel was

Driving on tires wrapped in cloth, Horace Thomas pilots the Old's Pirate in the first race on the beach in Daytona. Motorsports Images & Archives Photo

torn down in 1992, four years after celebrating its 100th birthday, and replaced by a condominium.

In its early years, however, the Hotel Ormond served as the cornerstone of the community's meager tourist industry and was the hub of most of the community's social activities. Many events took place on the 100 yards of cypress-planked veranda, which stretched along the south side of the facility. Every important social leader who visited the area stayed there, including oil magnate John D. Rockefeller. He eventually purchased a mansion across the street—called The Casements and now a city museum—and visited the hotel via an underground tunnel.

Flagler, who partnered with Rockefeller to monopolize the oil industry in the 1800s, had turned to commercial real estate in his later years and was responsible for helping develop Jacksonville, West Palm Beach and Miami. Some of the tourists his trains carried to sunny Florida included pioneers in the fledgling automobile industry.

By then, racing had already gained a foothold in other parts of this country. While there weren't hundreds of races around the country every week, the few that had been held clearly demonstrated public interest. In 1894, Count De Dion won the first auto competition on a 78.75-mile road course between Paris and Rouen in France, driving at an average of about 11.6 mph. Some 19 cars participated in the event, which drew international attention. In 1895, Emile Levassor won the first long-distance race, averaging 15 mph on solid tires for the 740-mile jaunt between Paris and Bordeaux. In that race, Jules Michelin, who

founded his namesake tire company in 1888 to create bicycle tires, tried to get drivers to use newly invented pneumatic tires for cars, but when everyone declined, he built his own car and entered it. Levassor thought Michelin's puffy tires were stuffed with cotton and demanded proof that air was inside. Someone promptly performed a field test with an ice pick.

In this country, on Thanksgiving day in 1895, J. Frank Duryea outraced several competitors from the heart of Chicago, Illinois 27.18 miles south to Evanston, then back through the snow to win in seven hours and 17 minutes, an average speed of 7.5 mph. His feat, too, attracted wide interest.

In 1901, an unknown, would-be car manufacturer, Henry Ford, demonstrated the importance of racing. He went one on one with Alexander Winton, a Scotsman who was then this country's foremost auto racer, in a 10-mile race in Grosse Point, Michigan. According to published Ford Motor Co. promotional material, Ford had never raced against another car and had failed in several previous attempts to start a car-manufacturing company. His vehicle, nicknamed Sweepstakes, was seriously out-powered. Race cars in those days normally had about 40 horsepower. Winton's car topped 70 horsepower. Sweepstakes had two cylinders and produced 26 horsepower.

However, Ford was hoping to demonstrate to the public that an efficient, lightweight car could outperform a big car. There was a lot at stake for him. The family car he eventually produced for worldwide use, the Model T, also generated 26 horsepower.

The most famous driver of his day, Alexander Winton competed in the first beach race in this Bullet in 1903, lost and went home to complain that the sand was too slow. Motorsports Images & Archives Photo

After other competitors dropped out prior to the start of the race, only Ford and Winton were left. The race length was reduced to accommodate the limited number of entries. While Ford fumbled through the early part of the abbreviated event, Winton led seven of the 10 laps and built up a big lead. Then, his engine started sputtering. Ford even-tually passed him in front of the 8,000 fans in the grandstands that day and went on to win with an average speed of 45 mph.

The victory was worth $1,000 and a cut-glass punch bowl. More importantly, the unlikely win caught the eye of several financial investors who helped Ford start what became the Ford Mo-tor Company in June 1903.

The City of Daytona Beach set up this publicity shot in 1905 to show the width of the beach. Residents brought their cars onto the sand for the photographer. Motorsports Images & Archives Photo

Bob Burman, who would later set a speed record on the beach, posed in his stripped-down Buick in 1908 beside an airplane in another publicity shot. Motorsports Images & Archives Photo

Naturally, even folks in distant Florida were intrigued by the possibilities of racing. Cars had been on the beach since C. W. Seamans drove onto the sand in 1900. Bike races had been held for several years as well.

A year after Ford was making a splash on the race track, C. W. Birchwood, a winter resident, wrote a letter to *Automobile Magazine,* which was published in its December 1902 issue. Birchwood extolled the virtues of driving—and racing—on the beach and wondered why no one else realized it.

The article attracted the attention of J. F. Hathaway, a Massachusetts native who was another winter resident of Florida. A retired businessman,

Hathaway, who owned a Stanley Steamer, had already considered the concept. He noted that bicycle tracks left little impression on the sand, and began to send pictures and enticing articles to various automobile journals to try to drum up support for races. He also drove around Ormond Beach, incurring the wrath of at least one resident who labeled the car "a hell cart," according to a history of Ormond Beach. Author Alice Strickland said Hathaway's car later got stuck in the ocean and had to be pulled from the waves by a horse.

"Senator" William J. Morgan, a writer for *Automobile Magazine,* liked the idea enough to journey to Daytona Beach in February 1903. A native of South Wales who emigrated to Pennsylvania as a teenager, Morgan had picked up his nickname after hastily substituting for an actual U.S. senator who missed a speaking engagement. The loquacious journalist talked his magazine into funding his trip and, later, to sponsoring races on the beach.

Morgan did know something about racing, having sponsored a bike race on the beach in 1902, according to Strickland.

That's where the Hotel Ormond comes in. Hotel managers Joseph Price and John Anderson were always investigating ways to promote their facility. Ormond Beach was still considered "one thousand miles from anywhere," as one New York newspaper described it. In February 1903, Morgan met with Price and Anderson, whose name graces the tree-lined road that runs along the river to the west of the hotel's former site. He proposed running races on the beach on the theory that the people who came to the event would want to stay in the best accommodations. After all, a car was still a luxury item in those days. Only wealthy people owned them. Indeed, the races were originally limited to invitees only, so that "undesirable drivers and freak machines" would be "shut out," according to Strickland. That wouldn't change until 1905.

The two managers loved the idea of a car race. As a result, racing came to Ormond as a promotional gimmick for the sprawling, wooden hotel.

With "Senator" Morgan running the show, plans fell into place quickly. In March 26, 1903, barely a month after the initial discussions, the first beach races were held. Limited records have helped to muddy what should be a clear picture. Some historians, including NASCAR's Tuthill, have insisted the first race was actually held in 1902. So did Strickland.

Automobile Magazine said that the competitors "came back" in 1903 for the first officially sanctioned races. However, detailed studies by several writers, including Dick Punnett, an Ormond Beach resident, proved that the most famous participant, Alexander Winton, did not build the car he raced until mid-1902, too late to have participated in a spring race the previous year.

A history of Oldsmobile published on the Internet also gives the 1903 date.

The first Daytona races lasted three days and were an immediate success, despite some early mix-ups in communication. Hoping to establish credibility, Morgan tried to get the Jacksonville Automobile Association to sanction the event prior to the first green flag. He did not consider that local residents would form their own sanctioning body for the same purpose. As a result, Daytona Beach community leaders were furious with Morgan for bringing in an outside group to authorize the races. They threatened to block all activities. An array of apologetic telegrams softened any anger. Unfortunately, news of the confrontation had led to a cancellation announcement. Morgan acted quickly to send out news releases that the races were still on, but the damage had only been mitigated. Some drivers, caught in the middle and unsure whether or not to show up, simply stayed home.

Despite the limited field, the beach welcomed its first racers March 26.

That morning, the drivers drove onto the sand in Ormond Beach near what is now the end of East Granada Boulevard to start the time trials, heading south for Daytona Beach guided by poles—paid for by automobile pioneer Ransom Olds—placed every half mile to record distances. On the second day, the route was reversed because of inclement weather in the Ormond Beach area. The third day, Ormond Beach again was the starting point. Special timing equipment was brought in to make sure results were accurate.

Today, the Ormond Beach entrance on A1A is paved near the site of the vanished hotel and located off busy Granada Boulevard. A modern inn sits on the south side of the short entry with public facilities and a small park to the north. In 1903, none of that was there. Since there were only two hotels in the city—both owned by Flagler—the beach seemed desolate with vegetation covering the low dunes. Participants dressed in suits. Women spectators, clad in long dresses, described as "hideous motoring costumes" by *Motor World,* carried parasols, while the men were formally attired. No one ever seemed to smile. Apparently, racing was serious business.

For the most part, drivers competed against the clock, not each other. Olds, one of the first to be timed, told Winton, "You have no idea, Alex, what a thrill it is out there. Do you know what it feels like to go 50 miles an hour?" The comment was quoted by author William Neeley, who credited it erroneously to 1902 instead of 1903.

Hathaway also got into the act in 1903, driving his Stanley Steamer on two runs. Oscar Hedstrom, the Swedish-born chief designer of motorcycles for Hendee Manufacturing, made a single lap on an Indian motorcycle "straight as an arrow" according to a report published in 1903. He stopped the clock at 1:09, breaking the one-mile, motorcycle-speed record set in Staten Island, New York, the previous spring. Sand, however, clogged and snapped his chain, ending his effort after one ride.

Later, W.W. Austin won the "championship of Florida" after posting a time of 1:36 on his Indian motorcycle.

Raymond Boothroyd, a Hotel Ormond guest, was timed at 1:28.4 to win a sprint between three Oldsmobiles—then the most popular car in the country and sold under the memorable song "My Merrie Oldsmobile." Ironically, Oldsmobile, the second oldest nameplate in automobile history behind Mercedes, ceased production recently.

None of the competitors were actually race drivers. Two were simply local doctors wealthy enough to own cars.

The drivers quickly noted several benefits of driving on sand. First, there was no choking dust to fly up and infiltrate engines or to blind drivers and spectators alike. Moreover, the slightly damp surface actually helped cool the tires, reducing stress. On the other hand, tires tended to slip on the uneven surface. Winton, fresh from his loss to Ford, created treads by cutting notches in his tires. The most famous driver of his day, Winton in 1896 had sold the first gasoline-powered engine in this country.

His opponent, Horace Thomas, an engineer

GETTING THERE

Intrepid travelers visiting Daytona Beach for the races in the first years of the 20th century had two choices—train or boat. No one drove until 1904, when Mr. and Mrs. William R. Hill decided to go that route. Their mishaps help explain why driving remained a rare option until several years later.

The couple started in Jacksonville and easily made the 42 miles to St. Augustine in about four hours. They needed a lot more time to cover the final 48 miles.

They intended to leave St. Augustine at daylight the next morning, but were delayed by rain until 10 a.m. For the first five miles, they drove their Knox down a shell-covered road to Moultrie, "where they were at once plunged into sand which was covered for a few miles by pine straw," according to an article in the February 4, 1904, issue of *The Automobile*.

The Hills doggedly moved to the Coopersville Road, then onto the King's Road. By that time, it was late in the afternoon. They were hoping to stay with Charles Duryant, but had to retrace their steps because of high water. The King's Road had been cut up by logging crews and inundated by water.

They ended up continually getting lost because "many of the intersecting roads were more traveled than the direct road and were misleading."

By the end of the second day, they had covered 30 miles and found refuge in the house of a Mr. Sterker.

They started the next day at 7 a.m., following their host, who had the good sense to ride a horse. Within a mile, "we were in muck up to our hubs," Hill later wrote a friend, "which meant getting men and plank to lift." That took about 90 minutes and must have seemed a pleasure compared to what followed. The Hills were introduced to the worst Florida had to offer—more mud, water, palmetto shrubs and wire grass estimated to be five feet high. At one point, the car got so stuck, Sterker had to go back and get a second mule for enough power to extricate it.

Properly exhausted, they paused to eat the lunch that had been saved from the day before.

Pushing on, they drove the car through a stream and found themselves entangled in a palmetto forest on the other side. "It became necessary to go ahead and cut a path before the wagon could go through," Hill reported. By 2 p.m., they had made enough room to continue and soon struck an old road, which was overgrown. They could motor through that and came within a half mile of the beach.

Then, things really went downhill. They found some gullies, a few more than a foot deep, which had to be filled in before the Knox could proceed. Finally, at 3 p.m., the Hills reached the shore about 30 miles north of Ormond Beach. They had needed eight hours to travel five miles.

They expected to drive on the hard-packed surface to Ormond Beach, only to discover they had arrived at high tide.

Sterker then decided to return home, and the Hills cautiously steered onto the sand. Still wet from the tide, it couldn't hold the car. They had to stop every few feet, jack up the car and pack sand under the wheels to gain traction before resuming.

They finally ran out of sunlight. "We removed and carried everything portable to the top of the sand barriers," Hill continued. Taking their car headlights and a hatchet, a precaution against animals, they hiked back to a hunting camp they had passed. They found food and were sent to a dredge working on a canal between the Halifax and Mantanzas Rivers. There, they set up camp and built a campfire. Hill went back to his car with four strong volunteers and moved it further away from the tide. Good thing. The next day, they found the car had spent the night only one foot from the high-water mark.

They reloaded, bought gasoline from the dredge supply and started south, covering the remaining 30 miles in about two hours.

Not the least scarred by their adventure, the couple announced plans to drive on to Miami when the beach races ended.

Every type of transportation known to man was brought to Daytona Beach's shoreline in 1903 as the city began to promote itself as a tourist and racing destination. Motorsports Images & Archives Photo

Drivers line up for the start of the 1905 races on the beach. Motorsports Images & Archives Photo

substituting for the delayed automobile pioneer Ransom Olds, opted to wrap his tires in cloth. He then set a new record in his Oldsmobile at 1:16.2 minutes.

By the time the third day of racing dawned, March 29, published reports had enticed thousands of spectators to fill in the soft sand away from the track.

"By 10 o'clock, the balconies and the long flights of steps up to the Coquina Hotel and the bathing pavilions were filled with ladies in the handsomest of light spring attire, while among them were men for a large part in straw hats and summer flannels. The entire country around and nearby Daytona had contributed scores of beach wagons and a dozen automobiles. Bicycles were on every hand. Winter tourists had stayed over for the automobile races, and the crowd at the start numbered fully a thousand. A hundred or more gathered at the finish line. Between them were scattered wagons and small groups," *Automobile News* recounted.

The wagons caused delays by repeatedly running over the timing wire and damaging it. Eventually, a new battery was also needed for the balky timer.

On March 28, 1903, Winton wheeled his Bullet #1 to the start line to drive against Thomas in an Olds Pirate for the initial Ormond Challenge Cup.

Neither car featured any bodywork. Winton "sat in a bucket-type seat mounted forward from the rear axle." The steering column was installed perpendicular, very close in design to a right angle. The motor was suspended beneath the chassis with the radiator square, mounted very low in the front. The in-line engine was placed on its side and had only one forward speed."

The Pirate "appeared to be simply arched steel

leaf-springs attached to a square steel front and rear axles to form a chassis. The wheels were bicycle-type with steel spokes. The springs supported two rocket-shaped tanks riding above the machine, mounted between the springs and about mid-way of the length of the peak of the arch. The engine was water-cooled and carried a radiator mounted at its front, all to the rear of the front axle." The driver "sat in a small plywood seat, his feet resting on two metal pads. One is reminded of a harness racing sulky, but one with four wheels."

Thomas lowered wind resistance by leaning forward in his seat.

"Senator" Morgan, ever a promoter, described the Pirate as a "long, sleek, rakish-looking craft."

When the starter gave the signal to go, Thomas pressed on the accelerator and chugged away. Winton gave him a 50-yard head start before lurching forward.

"It was a glorious chase to watch from the bathhouse steps," *Automobile News* reported. "The Bullet caught the Pirate just before the finish was reached and beat it by 1.5 of a second in 1:15." Other reports said the two men agreed to call the race a tie, although still insisting the race took place in 1902.

Ormond Beach received the nickname of "The Birthplace of Speed," while Winton took home the trophy.

The three days of events rewrote history, according to *Motor Age* magazine.

"The following new records have been established:

- A world's mile and world's kilometer record for medium, or light weight motor bicycles
- An American one-kilometer record for heavy cars—over 2,000 pounds.
- An American one-mile and kilometer record for light cars—under 1,000 pounds
- A 10-mile world's record for heavy cars made and likely to be accepted
- An unofficial but probably none the less actual world's five-mile record for heavy cars."

The publication immediately heaped on accolades. "Such a set of accomplishments—hardly needs comment or argument to convince the automobilists of the world that the beach on the Florida east coast lies the greatest natural motor vehicle speedway and race course in the world."

Chimed in *Automobile News,* "A new crop of American straightaway records and the organization of the Florida East Coast Automobile Association is the net result of three days of racing and speed trials on the Daytona-Ormond Beach that ended today. So successful was the tournament that it has been decided to make it an annual affair, and an association for that purpose was formed yesterday to absorb the Daytona and Seabreeze Associations and hold a week's tournament in the winter."

Racing in Daytona Beach was on its way.

chapter two

THE END OF
A DECADE

The success of the 1903 races initiated a series of "beach festivals," as one publication called them, and swathed the first decade of the 20th century with a collage of racing milestones and occasional pratfalls. **For the ensuing seven years,** men only recently introduced to mechanized motion began to push the limits of their machines across the smooth, hard sand of Daytona Beach.

Few nameplates on the automobiles have survived the years. It was not uncommon to have all the entries representing different manufacturers. Only the desire for speed remained a constant.

First, however, "Senator" Morgan had to overcome a major hurdle that threatened to throw a roadblock into the era only days after the echoes from the 1903 event had faded.

Hired by the newly formed Florida East Coast Automobile Association to run the 1904 version, Morgan began to read media accounts that foreshadowed a disaster. Alexander Winton, the best-known competitor from the previous year, went home disappointed by his results and promptly told newspaper reporters that the sand was too slow and that he could do better on a paved surface. He cited his effort in June 1902 on a Cleveland street, which, he said, was a full 10 seconds faster than his best time on the beach.

Winton's complaint circulated widely and generated a chorus of agreement, all from nonparticipants who couldn't believe sand could be solid enough to support sufficient speed. Faced with a serious public relations problem that could permanently suspend all beach rac-

Lewis Strang, a factory Buick driver who would go on to become famous, warms up his car prior to the 1908 Sandfest. Motorsports Images & Archives Photo

ing, Morgan approached the Packard Motor Company and suggested the company try out its Gray Wolf in Daytona. The car was of a medium weight (limit of 1,430 pounds) and had performed inconsistently in races earlier in the year. As a result, Packard officials were eager to redeem their car and their reputation. They jumped at the offer. The Stevens-Duryea Co. asked to join the time trials with a car that weighed less than 1,000 pounds. Since the vehicles were in different classes, Packard agreed.

The Stephens-Duryea Spider arrived first, showing up on December 30, 1903. The crates containing the Gray Wolf somehow were misplaced en route and were finally tracked down in Tennessee, mixed in with some cotton bales.

The Spider was little more than a flat piece of metal with four wheels and an engine. The design was admittedly improvised, according to designer J. Frank Duryea, and was based on another car in the Stevens-Duryea lineup. In a strange effort to improve stability, its tires were glued to the rim. The driver, Otto Nestman, was completely exposed, bending over the steering wheel as though opening a manhole. The Gray Wolf, on the other hand, resembled a motorized wedge of cheese with a more familiar steering wheel placed comfortably in front of driver Charles Schmidt, who, despite his name, was French. The name of the car was apropos, said Beverly Rae Kimes, writing in *Automobile Quarterly*. "The car appeared to be crouched, and its narrow snout was decidedly wolfish."

It featured a two-speed transmission, 34 x 3.5-inch wire wheels, a light, pressed-steel frame and weighed 1,310 pounds

While crews were assembling the newly located Gray Wolf, Nestman sent the Spider spinning down the beach on New Year's Eve in a record time of 57.2 seconds. The next day, January 1, 1904, he set the five-mile record in 4:57.4. The glue holding the tires onto the rims didn't survive that kind of stress, however. Nestman stopped the car when he could see air between the rubber and the rim. He wisely left the beach to Schmidt and had the Spider shipped to a New York auto show.

The Gray Wolf promptly loped to a new record for the five-mile course, easily bypassing Winton's previous effort in the process. In fact, the car even shattered ex-bicycle racer Barney Oldfield's circular track record, which had been set in a heavier car.

Nevertheless, Packard officials thought the Gray Wolf still had some hidden speed and were not pleased with the condition of the sand. The beach was considered "washboardy" during the initial runs, according to *The Automobile*. The car "had bounded about considerably, the wheels appearing to be off the ground half the time." They also thought the weather was not ideal, preferring a gale that would push the car down the course.

They got their wish. On January 3, the wind picked up, dropping the temperature from 70 to 50 degrees in 12 hours. With the strong breeze behind him, Schmidt raced down the beach to set new world and American records in the middle-weight class and almost topped the one-mile world's record, even though the Packard had only 24 horsepower compared to the much larger and more powerful Mors that set the benchmark.

The results silenced Winton and guaranteed the annual races, scheduled to begin at the end of January 1904, would wow any critics. They certainly did.

"Viewed from almost any standpoint, automobile races on the beach in Florida are a success," *The Automobile* gushed in its February 6, 1904 issue. "Imagine a perfectly straight speedway reach away as far as the eye can see without a break and nothing to distract the drivers' attention from his car; on one side the broad Atlantic and on the other, one hundred feet away, the loose sand beyond the tide line. Smooth as a billiard table and hard almost beyond belief is this magnificent stretch of beach. Nowhere in the world can be found a race course on which the driver of a mile-a-minute automobile can feel a greater sense of freedom and security."

The publication noted that the beach "is so hard that the heaviest machines make no impression in the sand, and so smooth that even going a mile in forty seconds there is almost no road vibration."

The emphasis on safety and a smooth ride was no coincidence. In 1902, two spectators were killed watching an attempt by a Baker Torpedo to set a one-mile speed record on a Staten Island street. A year later, and less than three weeks before the Daytona Beach festivities, Henry Ford had tried to test his new Model B on a frozen lake. He set a

record for the mile at 39.4 seconds, but almost skewered himself and mechanic Ed Huff in the process.

The gentle surf and soft sand on both sides of the Florida "shell" course had to seem more appealing than hard walls and metallic viewing stands.

At least 15 cars showed up to race in 1904, led by William K. Vanderbilt, Jr. He was typical of the entrants. Called "gentleman drivers," they were wealthy and enjoyed the competition while mechanics got their hands dirty to keep the cars running. Only a few of the competitors could be called professionals. Automobiles were still too new and too expensive.

Then 25 and the grandson of Cornelius Vanderbilt, who had built the family fortune, Vanderbilt Jr. drove a Mercedes (named for the eldest daughter of car designer Emil Jellinke) with the driver's seat higher than the seat occupied by the mechanic. The car also featured wooden-spoke wheels and a chain drive, which was noisy, needed regular lubrication and had the nasty habit of spraying globs of oil on spectators.

Because of various complications, Vanderbilt, Jr. started on his record attempt late in the day. As a result, there wasn't enough time to set up the timing equipment, so several judges armed with stopwatches took up positions at the start and finish lines.

Despite needing about 1.5 miles to pick up sufficient speed, Vanderbilt Jr. posted an astonishing 39-second mile, eclipsing Ford's icy effort. He

In its heyday, the Stanley Steamer was the fastest car on the beach. The man in the white coat is famed driver Fred Marriott. Motorsports Images & Archives Photo

then ran against Barney Oldfield, only to lose in a thick haze. It was a brief setback. The crankshaft in Oldfield's car broke, leaving the field to Vanderbilt Jr., who promptly set world records for all distances from five to 50 miles.

With that effort, Daytona Beach established its ranking as the top spot for speed in the world.

One unidentified reporter, quoted in Strickland's book, said in 1904: "All these race records have demonstrated that the 15-mile course on the Ormond Daytona Beach is the greatest automobile speedway in the world, natural or artificial. And, it is likely to be the Mecca of all time for the makers, designers and drivers desiring to test the speed of the automobiles they build, design or pilot. A journey across the ocean be found none too long or expensive for European builders, drivers and designers to test the speed of their motor vehicles on now what is the standard course in the world."

Given the panegyric nature of the work, Morgan probably wrote that text.

The following years were more hectic and beset with an array of problems.

The most chaotic of the early meets, the 1905 races, were held in unseasonably cold conditions made more aggravating by complete confusion. Promoter Morgan, who twisted his ankle and watched most of the 1904 events from his room, was fired by the new leaders of Florida East Coast Automobile Association who wanted to transfer the events to Daytona Beach—then, as now, a larger community—from Ormond Beach. Parochial interests motivated them, not convenience, because,

unfortunately, the racers and their staffs insisted on staying in those luxury accommodations in Ormond Beach. Eventually, a compromise was worked out. The starting line shifted from one city to the other day to day.

To compound the unsettled situation, none of the new officers had any experience in running an event like this. As a result, races were often delayed, creating a severe hardship for drivers shivering in open cockpits. One early-morning start was washed out when one officer misguessed the onset of low tide. Everyone stumbled out of bed at 7 a.m. only to discover that the course had disappeared under water. "It is safe to assume the errant mathematician also disappeared," author Punnett wrote.

There was also a tragedy. Frank Croker, the son of an infamous Tammany Hall politician who had fled to Ireland in the wake of corruption charges, was testing his 75-horsepower S & M Simplex racer on the beach with mechanic Alexander Raoul when their car collided with motorcyclist Newton Stanley, nephew of the twin brothers who produced the Stanley Steamers. Stanley apparently lurched to the side to avoid a wave, but did not see Croker, who was forced to swerve abruptly but did not clear the motorcycle. The impact sent Croker's car flipping over several times before stopping in the ocean. Stanley suffered a broken leg, but Raoul was killed instantly. Croker died the next day.

The races went on despite the accident. Five drivers set world records, including an English chauffeur, Arthur McDonald, who drove his employer's car. Herbert L. Bowden, a felt manufacturer, made the biggest impact. Annoyed by his failures in 1904, he tied a four-cylinder engine from his Mercedes to an identical engine borrowed from his boat. The combination elongated the hood, so that his car looked like a hot dog on wheels, but it helped him set a new standard for a one-mile run.

Louis Ross also created a stir with his 20-horsepower steam engine, which resembled a low-slung, 1940s, open-wheel roadster with a pointed nose. *Motor World* described it as a "turtle-shaped thing with its stubby smokestack pointed upward and rearward, suggesting that a devil-possessed turtle is skimming the earth hind-end foremost." It "vomited steam all over the gasoliners." Equipped with two, unconnected engines, Ross had to operate both throttles simultaneously while steering. As a result, his course was understandably erratic. Nevertheless, he upset three factory-built cars to win the Thomas Dewar Trophy for the one-mile run. Vanderbilt Jr. was among the losers. Very upset, he never returned to race in Florida.

Ross' entry bore the No. 4, the beginning of numbered entries. Ford had 999 painted on the side of his car, but that was a carryover from another car's name, not an identifying number.

Overall, 42 cars participated in 28 events during seven days of racing.

Embarrassed by the various missteps, officials formed a new organization to oversee the races and re-hired "Senator" Morgan to make sure everything ran smoothly in 1906. They were also fearful of competition. During these early years, beach races were held in three other communities: Newport, Rhode Island (1904-05); Atlantic City, New Jersey (1905-1906); and Cape May, New Jersey (1905). The times recorded there were not comparable to Florida's "wonder beach," but did make organizers aware that their grip on this type of racing was tenuous at best.

Morgan's experience paid off. The seven days of activities in 1906 unfolded smoothly, although not all the drivers were as accommodating. Auguste Hemery, who won the 1905 Vanderbilt Cup, was already known for his fiery temper and had caused disruptions in European races. He grew incensed when his Darracq was disqualified for being overweight. That was remedied only when it was discovered that the entry form had a misprint. He still had to find a way to pare 14 pounds before being allowed to compete. Later, Hemery was outraged when a false start forced officials to throw out the results of a race he apparently won.

Finally, convinced he had little chance to beat Fred Marriott and his Stanley Steamer, Hemery pulled into line next to Marriott's wood-and-canvas car. He positioned his open exhaust stacks toward the Steamer, then revved his engine. The resulting sparks blackened the Steamer's side, but didn't set it afire.

Eventually, Hemery was permanently suspended by race officials, then dismissed by Darracq Co., although his career continued with great success in Europe. His seat was eventually taken by Louis Chevrolet, a professional driver who had been brought to Florida by J. Walter Chrysler, an early car manufacturer. The Swiss-born Chevrolet would go on to create a company that still bears his name, even though he was bought out early on after a dispute with his partner.

The 1906 meet belonged to the Stanley Steamers, much to the disgust of the other drivers. Historian Tuthill said that when the steam car beat the Mercedes gasoline entries, it was like an "interloper defeating a local hero."

The cars were the product of a company started by twin brothers, F.E. and F.O. Stanley, from Massachusetts. They saw racing as a way to promote their products. Their entry resembled an "upside down canoe." That was an apt description. The Stanleys made some early tests of wind resistance by dragging various canoes through city streets behind a trailer. They turned the best design into a car.

Their Model H Gentlemen's Speedy Roadster was labeled the "Fastest Stock Car in the World" after winning a 15-mile race at 68.18 mph. Its closest competitors were four to five minutes behind.

Marriott, a foreman in Stanley Co.'s repair department, was the dominant driver. His Steamer, variously known as Teakettle, Beetle, Wogglebug and Rocket, among other names, featured a two-cylinder engine mounted in the rear and geared directly to the rear axle. Its boiler was held in place by a mile of steel wiring capable of withstanding 1,000 pounds of pressure. In a practice run, Marriott found his car reared up and carried him on two wheels for 20 yards before being stopped. That was remedied by adding extra weight in front.

The Steamer did have one drawback. The water in its boiler had to be heated to create steam, a process that could take five to 10 minutes. After ignition switches were invented in 1912, eliminating cranks, drivers didn't want to wait for the steam.

The days of the Steamer were numbered; the company would go out of business in 1925. Before that, though, the steamers and the gasoliners waged a fierce battle.

In 1906, the Steamers won. Marriott even suffered a cracked casing in one race and tried to coast the final two miles of a race. Having built a huge lead, he ended up losing by only 200 yards.

There were a few mishaps. Joe Tracy was hired to drive a Peerless, but was plagued by broken universal joints. The last joint broke when the car was stuck in the sand at low tide. It couldn't be removed and was dunked when the tide rolled in. A Columbia, which broke its own differential trying to pull out the Peerless, "suffered a similar overnight bath," according to a brief biography of Tracy by Henry Austin Clark, Jr.

Glenn Curtiss, later to develop airplanes, showed off the fastest vehicle. His eight-cylinder, air-cooled motorcycle hit an astounding 136.364 mph for a mile, but the clocking was unofficial. Curtiss had no money for entry forms and slept beside the Ormond Garage, which had been built in 1904 by railroad tycoon Henry Flagler to accommodate racers. As a result, Curtiss had to cajole officials into letting him try out his machine. His run was not scheduled, and no one could agree if the timers holding watches had managed to record the time accurately. Curtiss's bike featured tucked-in handlebars that extended below the level of the gas tank. Lacking a transmission, it had to be towed up to 30 mph to start. The power came from a V-8 engine originally designed for a Wright brothers airplane.

AUTOMOBILE MANUFACTURERS

These days, car buyers can choose from a wide assortment of foreign and domestic manufacturers, including, but not limited to, Japanese (Honda, Subaru, Mazda, Toyota, Nissan, Mitsubishi); German (Mercedes-Benz, Volkswagen, Audi, BMW); Swedish (Saab, Volvo); Korean (Daewoo, Hyundai, Kia); English (Jaguar, Rolls-Royce); Italian (Fiat, Lancia, Lamborghini, Ferrari, Masserati); Yugoslavian (Yugo); and American, (Ford, Chrysler, General Motors).

Many of these companies are interrelated and often manufacture cars or parts for each other. For example, General Motors owns Daewoo; Jaguar is part of Ford Motor Co.

However bewildering the options may be these days, they do not compare to the welter of manufacturers offering cars for sale in the first part of the 20th century.

Some of the companies changed their marquees and continued production under new names. The Overland, for example, started production in 1903 and became the Whippet in 1926. The Toledo, Ohio, company went out of business in 1931 during the depths of the Depression.

Some of the companies merged with others. Oakland, which made cars until 1932 in Pontiac, Michigan, was bought out by General Motors and its name changed to Pontiac. Henry Leland produced cars under the Lincoln brand from 1917 to 1922. The company was purchased by the Ford Motor Co., which continued the marquee.

Some companies live on inside larger firms: Nash, Rambler and Hudson joined together to become American Motors, which is now part of Chrysler Corporation. Chrysler was subsequently purchased and is part of a German company now called DaimlerChrysler.

Naturally, the early years were the hotbed of automobile production. No new American car companies have started up inside the United States since the 1930s. Several Americans, such as John DeLorean, went abroad to create their own cars.

Here is a partial list of American companies that once proudly displayed their nameplates on American roads and—many of them—on Daytona's famed beach.

Year Started	Company	Year Started	Company	Year Started	Company
1893	Duryea	1903	Orient Buckboard	1912	Old Reliable
1897	Autocar	1903	Pope-Hartford	1912	Stutz
1897	Oldsmobile	1903	R.E.O. (Ransom E. Olds)	1913	Chandler
1897	Winton	1903	Speedwell	1913	Duesenberg
1898	Haynes	1903	Star	1913	Grant
1899	Adams-Farewell	1903	Overland	1913	Owens Magnetic
1899	James Flyer	1903	Calorie	1913	Vulcan
1899	Packard	1903	Chadwick	1914	Ajax
1899	Squier	1904	American Motor Co.	1914	Briscoe
1900	Auburn	1904	Darling	1914	Havoc
1900	Cleveland	1904	Maxwell	1914	Vim
1900	Cord	1904	Sturtevant	1914	Dodge Bros. Inc.
1900	Crestmobile	1905	Marion	1914	Hercules
1900	Elmore	1905	Moon	1914	Portland
1900	Knox	1906	Kissel Motor Car Co.	1914	Willy's-Knight
1900	National	1906	Success	1915	Daniels
1900	Peerless	1907	Cartercar	1915	Sun
1900	Stearns-Knight	1907	Heine-Velox	1916	Comet
1901	Equitable	1907	Metz	1916	Fageol
1901	Franklin	1907	Oakland	1916	Jordan
1901	Lozier	1908	Chalmers	1916	Liberty
1901	Pierce-Arrow	1908	E.M.F. (Everitt-Metzger-Flanders)	1916	Stevens
1902	Cadillac Automotive Company	1908	Hupmobile	1917	Biddle
		1908	Keeton Six	1917	Lincoln
1902	Holsman Auto Buggy	1908	Paige-Detroit	1917	Lone Star
1902	Locomobile	1908	Velie	1917	Vogue
1902	Marmon	1909	Alco	1918	Texas
1902	Queen	1909	Case	1919	Mutual
1902	Rambler	1909	Cole	1920	Leach
1902	Ricketts	1909	Hudson Motor Car Co.	1920	Preferred
1902	Stevens Duryea	1909	Ricketts	1920	Ranger
1902	Studebaker	1909	Simplex	1921	Chrysler
1903	Apperson	1910	Mercer	1921	Wills St. Clair
1903	Buick Motor Co.	1901	White	1922	Rickenbacker
1903	Chadwick	1911	Chevrolet	1926	Whippet
1903	Ford Motor Co.	1911	Cunningham	1927	Graham-Paige
1903	Mitchell	1911	Komet	1929	Ruxton
		1912	J.B. Rocket Cyclecars	1930	Vaux-Hall Motor Co.

Source: Archives, International Speedway Corp.

Interesting though that feat was, most of the attention was riveted by a 100-mile event between six drivers. Held on the sixth day of the meet, January 28, it was the automotive story of the year.

Englishman Walter Clifford-Earp and engineer H.H. Baker grabbed the early lead in their 80-horsepower Napier. The two men were nattily dressed in white racing garments, a color that could only be worn on a dust-free beach.

Chasing them were Italian teammates Emanuel Cedrino and Vincenzio Lancia in Fiats. Another Englishman, Hilliard, was in a Napier, while Chevrolet was behind the wheel of a Christie.

Earp was still ahead after 37 miles when his right rear tire exploded. He got out and calmly stripped off the remaining rubber and ran the rest of the race on its rim. He had actually practiced for such an emergency and was well aware that the sand would support the car, something that hard pavement would not have done. He also had wire wheels, which were stronger than the wood still used on many cars.

While Earp barreled along on three tires—to the amazement of spectators following the race—the other drivers began to fall away. Chevrolet found the surf and retired with water in the carburetor. Lancia dropped out with radiator problems and ended up on a lonely stretch of the beach. At about 70 miles, Cedrino found himself on the deserted part of the south beach with tire problems. Fortunately, Lancia was nearby. They shifted the good tires from Lancia's car to Cedrino's, and the race was on.

On four good tires, Cedrino was able to run down Earp, who was having trouble negotiating the seven curves on three wheels.

With the big crowd cheering Earp on, he managed to win by 50 seconds. However, he didn't know the race was over and kept going. He had to be flagged down and brought back to get his trophy.

That race and the 1906 festivities were the highlights of the coming years. The overwhelming success of the Steamers in 1906 dampened enthusiasm for the annual gathering. Worse, the major automobile trade show, held in Chicago, was also scheduled for the same time period. Very few drivers bothered to come to Ormond Beach January 21 through January 25, 1907. Morgan tried everything to entice interest, even including a glider and having trophies handed out by a local beauty queen.

Nothing worked. In the end, he cut the 1907 event in half from its usual eight days.

Only five cars signed up for the premier 100-mile race. One driver, L.H. Perlman ran out of gas en route. A friend pointed out two cans of fuel, which were quickly emptied into the gas tank. Perlman then discovered one of the cans contained water.

Friendly assistance had to be considered a major hazard those days. A Packard caught fire before the race in the Ormond garage. An onlooker, trying to be helpful, tossed some liquid onto the flames. Bad idea. It turned out to be gasoline. A yellow Hotchkiss parked nearby also caught fire and was unable to compete.

Another entrant, Ralph Owen, drove 19 days from New York to Daytona to enter the race. He clearly was not very serious about the effort. He came in last, but probably had a nice time chatting en route with his two female passengers.

E.R. Hollander's 120-mph Fiat Cyclone finally won the 100-mile race and received a $100 bonus from Continental Tires, the first effort by a parts manufacturer to cash in on motorsports. Company officials, however, had to be a bit embarrassed. Hollander barely made it to the finish line. He finished, like Earp the year before, on three wheels. A tire separated from the rim on two separate occasions and "proceeded merrily down the beach by itself," author Punnett reported.

S.B. Stevens finished second in the 125-mile race in 1:54:28. He ended up less than a minute behind winner Louis J. Bergdoll despite a 29-minute

wait in Daytona Beach to replace a broken rocker arm.

Pit stops have improved since then.

The "sandfest" would turn out to be the last hurrah for the Steamers. Marriott crashed, even though he was aware that the beach course was marred with several ruts. He felt that at proper speed, his car would be able to glide across the top of them. He was wrong. His car handled the first one with ease, but was tossed into the air by the second one. Marriott was traveling an estimated 150 mph at the time. The car was destroyed in the surf. Marriott was badly injured and taken to the nearby clubhouse where a local doctor plopped his distended eyeball back into place. Amazingly, his vision was unaffected.

Rivals tried to claim that Marriott's boiler blew up, but pictures of the shattered car show that

Englishman Walter Clifford-Earp (behind wheel) and engineer H.H. Baker powered to victory in the featured 100-mile race in 1906, although they drove the last part of the race without a right-rear tire. Motorsports Images & Archives Photo

was not true. Passersby actually picked up pieces of the car and sold them for souvenirs.

The Stanley brothers were so shaken by the accident that they completely pulled out of racing. The gasoline engines had won the war.

The route was complete in 1908. New rules banned cars that couldn't travel at least 100 miles at 60 mph. That effectively eliminated electric and steam entries. Still, few other cars showed up to test their abilities on the "far-famed, wave-washed sands" for four days of racing in March. Some of the 12 cars that eventually arrived never got onto the beach. A Cadillac ran into a tree and did not compete. Dr. Pittman's Buick went back to St. Augustine when the doctor received "a professional call home."

Morgan did everything he could to draw attention, including running a race from Jacksonville to Miami. A Cleveland Runabout spent six days marking the road, then returned to Daytona Beach.

The car apparently could handle the 270-mile trek, but not a brief jaunt on the beach. On the second day of racing, R.J. Kelsey borrowed the vehicle, ironically nicknamed the Pathfinder, and, hampered by fog, ran into the remains of an old shipwreck along the shoreline. The *Nathan T. Cobb* had gone down in the late 1800s and was the subject of a gripping account by famed writer Stephen Crane. There's still a marker on the beach to indicate the site. The car's owner, James Laughlin III, tried to have Kelsey arrested, but settled for an agreement to have the automobile repaired. There wasn't much left. It couldn't be retrieved for 24 hours and spent part of the night completely underwater.

Water also played a part in the primary race, a 256-mile run for the Automobile Club of America cup. Drivers completed eight circuits of 32 miles each, cut back from 288 miles because of the fear that the onrushing tide would swamp the course. By agreement, the winning Fiat continued on to complete 300 miles in 3.53:44.

With interest clearly fading, Morgan did everything he could to promote the 1909 events. He announced, among other things, that planes would be included, a dirigible was coming, and that famed woman driver Joan Newton Cueno would compete along with a host of world-class drivers.

None of that happened. Only one plane showed up, but the pilot never got it off the ground. The dirigible didn't float by. Few cars were on hand, either.

Morgan was fighting an impossible battle. The economy had dropped into a recession in 1908, leaving fewer competitors willing or able to make the expensive trip to Florida. The Indianapolis Speedway opened in 1909, creating a controllable setting for races as well as a way to collect admissions. The miles of open beach in Daytona made it impossible to limit spectators or charge for viewing. As a result, the Florida East Coast Automobile Association, which was underwriting the events, began to consider cancelling the annual races. In 1910, the group would actually announce the end, but would relent at the last minute.

An array of motorcycles did show up, adding a new flavor to the activities. In time, motorcycles would become as important to Daytona Beach's racing future as cars.

Cars, however, were the main attraction. There were only nine of them, but they produced seven records in eight events. The hard sand of Daytona Beach had lost none of its speed.

Italian-born Ralph de Palma led the way. In 27 years of racing, de Palma reportedly entered 2,800 races and won more than 2,000 of them, according to a biography by William F. Nolan. His car was the only entrant in the featured 100-mile race in 1910. De Palma, whose name lives on via a grandstand section at Daytona International Speedway, drove a couple miles and was declared the winner. When his car reached more than a mile in 40 seconds, it "bounced like a rubber ball, all four wheels at times leaving the ground," according to *Motor World*.

A year later, cigar-smoking Barney Oldfield returned to dominate a handful of events in a Blitzen Benz nicknamed "Lightning." *Motor World* called his performance, "the most startling flights against time ever made by a man and an automobile."

In the article, Oldfield described driving the Benz as "the sensation of riding a rocket through space." He also decided that "a speed of 131 miles per hour is near to the absolute limit of speed as humanity will ever travel."

J. Walter Christie, who had five different entries in five years, tried to be com-

petitive despite innumerable mechanical failures. After his driver was unable to finish two events in 1910, Christie took over the driver's seat. He removed a faulty radiator, packed the car with 100 pounds of ice and ran a mile in 33.15. It wasn't a record or good enough to revive Christie's hopes of producing a saleable car.

He abandoned racing that year and later tried to interest the U.S. government in some ideas he had to improve the performance of tanks. Europeans were more interested and followed his drawings. Christie eventually died destitute in 1944 while tanks based on his design were fighting World War II.

In 1910, he was among the handful of disappointed racers as the rising tide short-circuited the automatic timing apparatus and stopped planned mile trials and a 50-mile race.

The final day of the 1910 festivities featured a 300-mile race for the W.B. Five Thousand Dollar Trophy, which had been donated by the W.B. Corset Co. of New York. However, heavy rain forced the event to be cancelled and symbolically ended not only the four days of activities, but, possibly, Daytona Beach's position as the center of racing.

What had started with such promise in 1903 seemingly ended on a soggy afternoon under gray skies beside a raging sea.

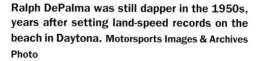

Ralph DePalma was still dapper in the 1950s, years after setting land-speed records on the beach in Daytona. Motorsports Images & Archives Photo

chapter three

SPEED KINGS

While the annual sandfests in Daytona Beach faded into memory, racing remained an integral part of daily life. After all, the beaches were still "smooth and as hard as a billiard table," as one magazine called them. The lure of setting a record guaranteed some brave driver would test his car against the clock in the ensuing years.

Actual beach races would not return until 1936. Instead, sleek vehicles built totally for speed began to dominate. They did not show up on a regular basis. Often, the foam balls had the beach to themselves for some mindless sprints. After all, it took years to design and construct a mechanized monster capable of hitting record speeds. But, when "Wild Bob" Burman, Ralph DePalma, Major Henry O'Neil de Hane Segrave and Malcolm Campbell became haunted by a vision of speed, the specter of Daytona's legendary past arose to startle the racing world.

Burman was first to try to break Oldfield's speed record. Born on an Iowa farm in 1884, he became a test driver in Michigan by 1901 and moved to the newly formed Buick Motor Co. Two years later to paint cars. Reportedly, Burman drove the first Buick ever made. By 1906, Burman was competing in races and soon was proclaimed as the "World's Speed King."

Buick's founder, William Capo Durant, believed that "the best way to sell cars was to race them." He hired brothers Louis and Arthur Chevrolet, along with Burman. Then, he entered

OPPOSITE: **Two giants in the early years of racing, Malcolm Campbell (left) and Barney Oldfield, share a few moments together in the 1920s.** Motorsports Images & Archives Photo

Bob Burman, shown here after setting the world land-speed record in 1911, was one of many daredevils drawn to the beach by the chance to go faster than anyone had done before. **Motorsports Images & Archives Photo**

the team in as many races as possible. As a result, Buick piled up an estimated 500 race trophies between 1908-1911.

Burman competed in the inaugural Indianapolis 500 in 1911, two years after Carl Fisher opened the facility.

"Wild Bob Burman is the equal of any driver in the world and, what's more, he's exciting," said E.H. "Ernie" Moross, a wily promoter who hired Burman to drive Barney Oldfield's Blitzen Benz. In a fit of anger, Oldfield announced he was retiring and sold off his cars. Moross promptly bought the Benz.

In 1911, Burman celebrated his 27th birthday on the beach at Daytona. As always, he drove in a business suit and tie with his cap reversed. After

uniforms were introduced, he still wore a silk shirt, bow tie and business trousers underneath. He had been in Daytona once before, racing a rickety bi-plane in a 1909 publicity stunt.

Oldfield, who unretired as quickly as he left the sport, was not convinced anyone could go faster than his speed record. Burman, who would be killed in a 1916 street race in California, disparaged that idea quickly, blowing by the 131 mph mark in prac-tice. Wind stirred up by his speed repeatedly blew out the lenses in his racing goggles. Burman merely riveted the lenses into place during breaks and kept driving.

On April 23, 1911, he clocked in at 141.132 mph. For good measure, Burman also set the two-mile and 20-mile records along with the one-ki-lometer record and the one-mile record from a standing start.

That feat augmented his growing reputation as America's finest driver.

"He did more to make automobile racing a real competitive sport than any other driver of my time," said driver Bill Pickens.

The American Automobile Association (AAA), which became the "self-proclaimed arbiter of all speed records" in 1902, certified Burman's time, but the Federation International de L'Automobile (FIA) in Paris declined. The AAA was not affiliated with the FIA, so no times turned in prior to an international agreement in 1927 made their way into the official international record book. It didn't matter. Burman's effort was so convincing that no one attempted to beat it for eight years.

That's when DePalma took up the challenge. He was probably best known then for a 1912 race

he didn't win. Competing in the second Indianapolis 500, DePalma had driven his famed Gray Ghost to a five-lap lead with only three laps left when his Mercedes started leaking oil after a broken connecting rod punctured the crankcase.

Crawling along at about 15 mph, DePalma, then 28, tried to nurse the stricken car into Victory Lane. Midway through lap 198, two laps from the checkered flag, the engine froze up. With sweat pouring down his face, DePalma and his mechanic, Rubert Jeffkins, then pushed the heavy car the rest of the way. DePalma was disqualified, but managed to capture the imagination of race fans, especially after he rushed over to be the first to congratulate the winner, Joe Dawson.

Raised in Brooklyn, N.Y., the Italian-born DePalma had become a professional bicycle racer by 1902. After an abbreviated race on a motorcycle— he illegally substituted for another driver and was banned for a year—DePalma turned to cars and was a flagman for the 1906 Vanderbilt Cup race on Long Island, New York.

In June 1908, he defeated Oldfield in a series of dirt-track heats held in Massachusetts. Oldfield never forgave the young upstart, and the two men feuded for another decade on and off the track. DePalma, who died in 1956, always said his greatest race was a victory over Oldfield in the 1914 Vanderbilt Cup held on the roads of Santa Monica, California, in front of 125,000 spectators. Despite having a much slower car, DePalma lured Oldfield

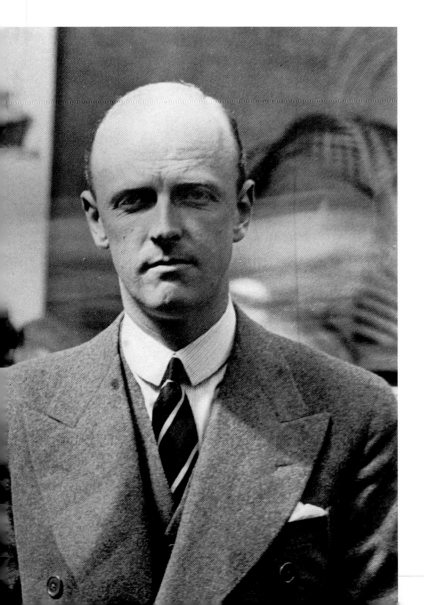

Englishman Henry Segrave was the first man to top 200 mph on the beach in Daytona. Motorsports Images & Archives Photo

into running his tires down to their nubs. When Oldfield had to pit, DePalma went on to win.

Their animosity was understandable: two racing heroes who came from different backgrounds and had completely opposite approaches to racing. Oldfield, who was stocky in contrast with the taller DePalma, was a consummate showman who raced proudly and openly only for money. Raised in poverty, the Ohioan repeatedly jumped from one manufacturer to another on the trail of dollar bills.

Hyperbole was Oldfield's middle name. "You have the sensation of being hurtled through space. The machine is throbbing under you with its cylinders beating a drummer's tattoo, and the air tears past you in a gale," he proclaimed in 1903 after driving 60 mph. "In its maddening dash through the swirling dust, the machine takes on the attributes of a sentient thing. I tell you, gentlemen, no man can drive faster and live."

Born Bernd Eli in 1878, Oldfield started racing bicycles and recorded a championship in 1894. He ran in his first automobile race in 1902 and later affected a gaudy, green-leather racing outfit for maximum attention. He also chewed on a cigar while driving, a habit adopted after damaging several molars in an accident.

His driving was unrestrained. "The rear wheels slide forward for a distance of 50 feet, throwing up a huge cloud of dirt," reported *The Automobile* in a profile of Oldfield published in *Smithsonian* magazine in 1998. "Men were white-faced and breathless, while women covered their eyes and sank back, overcome by the recklessness of it all."

Oldfield, who died in bed in 1946, raced against planes, trains and anything that moved, once appearing in a Mack Sennett movie thriller where he saved Mabel Normand seconds before disaster struck.

In contrast, DePalma was an immaculate dresser who was usually clad in white despite the dirt thrown up on many tracks. Deriding Oldfield as "the cigar-chewer," DePalma even insisted his mechanics maintain a high level of cleanliness. "They could never appear in public except in spotless attire," reported historian W.F. Bradley.

In 1919, back from World War I, where he served as a captain in the Air Corps, DePalma headed to Daytona Beach with a 12-cylinder, white Packard, with an airplane-prototype engine that featured a displacement of 905 cubic inches. A modern NASCAR NEXTEL Cup stock car, in contrast, has a 352-cubic-inch displacement. The Packard was designed with a square front and came to the point in back, sort of like a rocket ship aimed in the wrong direction.

The engine had already set aviation-and water-speed records, and had been used in several DePalma race cars. DePalma steered it to a new land speed record at 149.87 mph. The New Yorker spent a week in Daytona, shattering every other known record then available. As he was preparing to return home, someone remembered Burman's one-mile record from a standing start. That fell, too, at 92.71 mph.

DePalma's rampage through the record books juiced up the quest for the land-speed record. For the next 16 years, one driver after another came to Daytona Beach to aim for the title as the world's fastest driver. The sole object was to go fast. Records collapsed like sand castles pummeled by the tide. From 1922 through 1928, the land-speed record fell 14 times. Between 1904 and 1922, it traded hands on only eight occasions.

One year after DePalma's outburst, Tommy Milton showed up with mechanic Jimmy Murphy and a futuristic racer powered by dual Duesenberg engines. The car featured the first headrest and windshield (then called a "windscreen") used in racing. With pointed ends, the vehicle faintly resembled a 1950s Corvette. While his team prepared the car to try for the speed record, Milton took a quick trip to Cuba for a race there.

Born in 1893 in Minneapolis, Minnesota, Milton was blind in one eye—a fact he hid until near the end of his career—and was a superb mechanic. He began driving in 1913 and eventually would spurn a deal to buy Indianapolis Motor Speedway rather than forego what he thought would be a lucrative land investment. The 1929 stock market crash left him destitute. He worked for Packard for years before becoming chief steward of the Indianapolis 500.

Milton's race career would begin in 1913 and last for 12 years. This race in 1920 would be his finest hour, but Murphy almost ruined it while Milton was careening around Cuba. The car owners were concerned about the Duesenberg and wanted the young mechanic to give it a test run. Murphy, then 26, had been raised in California and given a motorcycle so he could commute to high school. Mechanically inclined, he dropped out of school soon after to open his own garage. He first drove a car in 1916 and was befriended by Milton.

While the boss was out of the country, Murphy set a new speed record in the practice run. The timers "just happened" to be set up to authenticate the new record, according to published reports.

Milton returned to be told about the record. He was outraged. "Can you imagine how I felt," he told Bill Tuthill for his 1978 *Speed on Sand* book, "learning that my car, built with my sweat and money, had been driven to a new world record by a fellow I had hired to get it ready for me?"

To make matters worse, if that were possible, Milton discovered that sand kicked up by Murphy's unauthorized trips down the beach had damaged the Duesenberg's powerplants. On his own, Milton pulled the car into a makeshift tent on the beach and completely rebuilt both engines.

He also fired Murphy, who then launched his own career by setting several Class C world speed records that year on the beach. In 1921, Murphy became the first American to win a European race. Ignoring intense pain from two broken ribs picked up in practice, Murphy also won the French Grand Prix. A year later, he came home first in the Indianapolis 500. His exploits won him enormous fame. Shortly after a dance was named for him, the "Jimmy Murphy Trot," he was killed in a 1930 race in California.

Four days after Murphy set his speed record, Milton was ready to try to break it. On April 27, 1920, he rolled onto the sand for his crack at the

HARD BEACHES

Why are the beaches along the Volusia County coastline hard enough to support race cars?

The answer came from an assistant state geologist who studied the beaches and published his report in 1930.

James H.C. Martens wrote that there were three basic reasons why the beaches were ideal for racing:

• Quartz content. The sand in Daytona Beach is almost exclusively quartz. In other areas, shells and pebbles are mixed in, creating an uneven surface. Shell fragments are also softer and smoother than quartz, proving little resistance to wheels. Quartz beaches extend from the Georgia-Florida border south to Cape Canaveral, although there are patches of softer sand along the way.

• Beach slope. A beach that slopes too steeply will not work. Martens noted that beaches along the northern half of Florida have a gentle slope. "The slope of the beach is so slight as to require practically no effort in steering an automobile parallel to the shore," he said. He credited that to the fine sand, which is carried from the north to the south. Coarse sand creates a steeper angle.

• Tide. "The greater the tide, the wider will be the strip of damp sand at low tide, the shorter will be the period when the beach is not suitable for driving," Martens said. The highest tides in Florida occur in Jacksonville. The size of the tides then decrease until they are less than two feet in Miami Beach.

The three elements come together in Daytona Beach to leave a wide stretch of hard, damp sand perfectly suited for sleek, fast cars.

Measured Mile. The fire engine siren sounded to alert residents of the coming effort. Spectators lined up along the sand dunes to watch. Milton revved up the engine, took the customary four-mile run to build up speed and started onto the course.

Immediately, a fire flared in the engine and began to shoot up through the hood louvers. Engulfed in flames, Milton refused to stop. Finally, after completing the mile, he moved closer to the ocean, hoping the waves would douse the flames without damaging the car. The ocean did its part, and he emerged slightly broiled with a new record of 156.046 mph.

The unofficial record didn't last long. Two years later, April 6, 1922, Sig Haugdahl, a champion dirt-track driver, visited the beach with a white, torpedo-shaped Wisconsin Special, which was also powered by a six-cylinder aircraft engine. A resident of Daytona Beach who had opened a local garage around 1920, Haugdahl was a member of the International Motor Contest Board, a rival of the AAA. Knowing whatever time he posted would be challenged, he set up an electric timing device and positioned a U.S. senator and the mayor of Daytona Beach as official observers.

They watched him jackrabbit across the sand at 180.27 mph.

With the elusive 200 mph benchmark finally within reach, the high-powered English drivers began their assault. They were led by Segrave, who,

In 1928, three racing legends met for the only time in a "high noon" showdown in Daytona Beach. Malcolm Campbell (left) beat Frank Lockhart (center) and Ray Keech in the race against the clock to set a land-speed record. Motorsports Images & Archives Photo

ACK HAW
'CIAL
DIANAPOLIS

Ralph Mulford made a test run on the beach in this Hudson in 1916. The car seems to lean forward because the camera shutter speeds then were too slow. **Motorsports Images & Archives Photo**

in 1927, brought a Sunbeam propelled by twin aircraft engines mounted in the front and rear of the driver. The Irishman had been warned that Americans would try to sabotage his effort, so he slipped into Daytona Beach with little fanfare. He quickly discovered that not only was his presence known, but local residents were happy to cheer him on.

His car arrived in crates, which was christened with a bottle of champagne by a local bathing beauty. While his polished, red entry was being prepared in what is now the Plaza Hotel garage, Segrave played golf with American star Walter Hagen and practiced an early-to-bed, early-to-rise training regimen.

His car weighed in at four tons, and its engine displaced an incredible 2,738 cubic inches. Segrave confidently announced the Sunbeam would

top 212 mph. He showed curious onlookers how the vehicle had been "machined and assembled with such precise accuracy that there was little chance of malfunction. There was no vibration," Neely said. Compressed air ignited the rear engine, which, in turn, started the front engine through a friction drive.

A typical nor'easter blew through Daytona Beach on March 28 with nonstop rain and chilling temperatures. Raging winds swept the beach, leveling it off and removing debris.

The following morning, "the siren in the Mainland fire station let loose with a long drawn scream," reported Fred Booth, then-associate editor of the *Daytona Beach Morning Journal*. "It brought out the National Guard, the police, the city engineers and the electricians, Sheriff's deputies, AAA officials with their timing devices."

The course started in Ponce Inlet, 12 miles to the south, and ended three miles south of the Main Street Pier, which is still standing despite being damaged by a hurricane in the late 1990s. Concrete markers had been placed in the dunes to mark every mile; colored flags were set up at 100-yard intervals. Segrave would have four miles to reach top speed before entering the Measured Mile, then four miles to cool down the engine.

By the time he was ready to pilot his Mystery S along the sandy route, most of the community had come to the beach. "They came in big cars and little ones, old and new," Booth recorded. "They came on bicycles and on foot. A few rode horses. They streamed across the bridges and along the streets leading to the beach. Women trudged, their skirts flapping in the smart wind, pushing perambulators. Boys came running and whooping, forgetful of the school hour not far off. Within the hour, the motley multitude peopled the dunes. From near the pier, along the length of the beach to the Inlet, they stood or sat. Thousands of men, women and children sat quiet, intent and waiting."

Breaking training, Segrave chain-smoked cigarettes and waited for word to start. Finally, Booth said, his car was towed to the south end. (Another source said he drove there, but Booth was an eyewitness.) Segrave put on a white leather helmet, setting a precedent. He wore it because no one

knew what might happen to exposed skin when winds sliced over the windshield at 200 mph. Helmets became the norm after Segrave's sprint.

The car sped up the course. "It loomed in the distance, then swooshed by and was gone from sight," Booth continued. "It didn't come thundering and shooting lightning from its tail. It made a humming sound like a huge top."

It also bottomed out below the magical 200-mph mark. Segrave and his four imported engineers and six mechanics pored over the car and found that shutters that could be opened at an angle to permit a flow of air into the rear engine had been closed for aerodynamics. As a result, the rear engine was not receiving enough air. That was easily remedied, and Segrave set off again.

Driving his red Sunbeam, oddly nicknamed The Slug, Segrave raced across Daytona's flat, hard sand at 200.668 mph. The G-force almost propelled him from the cockpit. When the brakes failed, he calmly drove into the sea. On the way back, now headed downwind, he topped 207.508 mph.

Segrave's average speed of 203.79 mph was almost 29 miles faster than the previous record.

That was good enough for him. Segrave made no more attempts and went home to be knighted.

The rest of the racing world, however, was not so complacent. An array of top drivers lined up determined to better his record.

Malcolm Campbell drove on silk tires that had a life of about seven minutes. Motorsports Images & Archives Photo

chapter four

END OF TIME TRIALS

The reverberations from Segrave's record-shattering run echoed internationally.

"It was a tremendous achievement," reported Richard Hough in his biography of Malcolm Campbell and his son, Donald, who was also a champion speedracer. "It also marked the opening of the most exciting, extraordinary combats in motoring history; a combat that took place, not over seconds or minutes hub-cap to hub-cap, nose to tail, on a Grand Prix circuit, but one that lasted for four years and, individually, on long, lonely stretches of sand thousands of miles from home."

He got the years wrong—the battle went on for seven years. That's all right; one writer who described the car races incorrectly reported Daytona Beach was situated next to the Gulf of Mexico, not the Atlantic Ocean.

The combatants who checked their maps before heading to Florida came from around the world to try their luck on the hard sands of Daytona Beach. An Egyptian millionaire, Prince Djellalledin, hired an Italian designer to come up with a competitive car, but it never topped 150 mph and dropped out of the running. British racing star Kaye Don was only able to reach 190 mph in an ill-handling Sunbeam Silver Bullet that frightened spectators and the driver alike.

OPPOSITE: **After blistering the sand at close to 300 mph, Malcolm Campbell's silk tires had to be discarded. Failure to change tires cost speed racer Frank Lockhart his life. Motorsports Images & Archives Photo**

Each competitor followed the same course. The measured mile was marked by rectangular yellow-and-black signs, strung on poles over the start/finish line. A tower to the west held timing and communication devices, while fans stretched along the dunes. The cars had to pass through the Main Street Pier pilings, which then extended 42 feet apart. Dotted black lines were painted on the sand with oil to help the driver spot the start and finish.

Malcolm Campbell began his attack on Segrave's record in February 1928. The son of a wealthy English diamond merchant and an insurance executive who made millions by inventing then selling libel insurance to newspapers, he had been attracted to speed as a youngster when he was given a motorcycle. In 1901, he was reportedly fined for dangerous driving after being spotted riding his bicycle at 27 mph with no hands on the handlebars. It's not clear who measured the speed or how.

As a young man, he had been charmed by Maurice Maeterlinck's classic play "The Blue Bird" about children eternally seeking joy in the world. The line about the "bluebird of happiness" struck Campbell's fancy, and he placed the phrase on his personal stationery, Christmas cards and his uniform. His race cars were all named Bluebird. There were an estimated 16 different editions, including the one now on permanent display inside DAYTONA USA. All were mammoth, from 25 to 30 feet long and weighing as much as five tons, and typically painted blue.

After a stint as a motorcycle dispatch rider and a pilot during World War I, Campbell decided to devote himself to setting speed records on land and water. His first attempts came in 1922, when he was already 37 years old. Speed may be a young man's attraction, but it became this older man's addiction. In 1928, he hurried to Daytona Beach af-

The start of the Measured Mile was indicated by a banner and marks in the sand. Motorsports Images & Archives Photo

The driver of the Bluebird essentially sat in the front of a small rocket. Motorsports Images & Archives Photo

ter hearing about Segrave's record. Deeply disappointed, Campbell had wanted to be the first to cross the 200 mph barrier and was determined to outdo any challenger to reach the next level.

Americans Ray Keech and Frank Lockhart were equally committed to the quest. They all came to Daytona Beach in February 1928 to compete. With three of the best known racers in the world gathered in one place, the moment was set for a dramatic face-off, a sort of "high noon" in the sands of Daytona Beach.

"It was the biggest event ever held in Daytona, and to the delight of the hotel and restaurant keepers and the Chamber of Commerce, a record crowd turned up to watch," recorded J. Wentworth Day, author of another Campbell biography.

Space was so limited that it cost four dollars a night for a mattress in a corridor or a blanket and pillow on a billiard table, published accounts noted.

When Campbell went out for his first test run early in the month, "the sandhills for miles were packed with people. They looked like masses of flies," Day reported. "Thousands of motorcars lined the courses, cameras clicked by the hundred, film photographers whirled their handles. A confused hum of voices, like the droning of bees, rose all down the long miles of the beach."

Campbell's first attempt was almost a disaster. His car hit a bump and went airborne for an estimated 30 feet before thudding to the ground. His staff needed days to repair the damage.

The Bluebird emerges from the shipping crate. Mechanics needed days to get the car in driving condition.
Motorsports Images & Archives Photo

On February 19, he tried again. "The drone of its engine grew to a roar, and like an airplane, it swooped down the beach into the measured mile, and shot past the crowd in a thunder of terrifying speed," Day wrote.

Campbell topped 214 mph on that first run before the Bluebird hit another bump and nearly destroyed itself during a terrifying half-mile struggle. The car "swept through the sand in a sideways skid, plowing it up in great waves," Day reported.

Pulling himself together, an exhausted, bruised Campbell made the return trip at about 199 mph, averaging a new world record of 206.95 mph.

"During a skid, I must confess, I had a momentary qualm," he told *Motor Sport*, an English publication, "but before I realized it, I had straightened out and was roaring onward down the course."

He also described his thoughts about traveling at such an incomprehensible speed. "My whole mind was concentrated on the task at hand, and my faculties were so riveted on one problem—keeping the Bluebird on her course—that I had no time for outside impressions," Campbell said. "The wind, of course, forced itself on my notice, and I have never conceived such a tremendous pressure of air, and I was thankful for the foresight that enclosed me in a cockpit. I hardly noticed the exhaust noise. The whole run was one tremendous sweep over sand, which I hardly felt, with a hurricane wind seeking to wrest the car from my control."

Then Lockhart, 25, took his turn at the starting line. Born in Ohio, he had been raised in California by his widowed mother. A lackadaisical student, he had shown immense mechanical skills as a child and built an engine for a Model T from parts supplied by a friend. He also competed in soap box derbies. Eventually, he carved out a reputation on California's dirt tracks. Boyish looking with light red hair, he came to Indianapolis in 1926 to watch a friend and was offered a ride when regular driver Peter Kreis became ill.

Driving recklessly in the rain, which allowed him to slide the way he drove the California dirt tracks, Lockhart built up a huge lead and was declared the winner when the race was called after 400 miles. As the first rookie winner of the Indianapolis 500, Lockhart, labeled the "boy wonder of racing," secured a place among American folk heroes of the era like Jack Dempsey and Babe Ruth.

Lockhart then shifted to speed racing, turning in a time of 171.02 mph on a dry California lakebed. That sparked the interest of investors. Fred Moscovics, owner of the Stutz Motor Car Co. of Indianapolis, loaned him money to build a car and to take it to Daytona. Armed with his first substantial bank account, Lockhart spared no expense. The Stutz was one of the first cars to be tested in a wind tunnel. Axles and wheels were streamlined. The car "was designed like a glistening white bullet" with rounded tire guards and a 181-cubic-inch engine. As a result, it became one of the most expensive built to date, costing reportedly at least $50,000 to $60,000. Estimates of the true price topped $100,000. Lockhart quickly ran out of funds and even named it the Stutz Black Hawk (also spelled Blackhawk), so Moscovics would give him more money.

Lockhart was offered $20,000 to drive on a set of tires not made by Firestone, his usual supplier. Needing cash, he agreed. It wasn't enough. Despite having several sponsors, Lockhart arrived in Daytona Beach deeply in debt.

As a result, he couldn't afford to sit around and wait for ideal weather. Although a nor'easter had sprung up, Lockhart insisted on setting out on February 22 despite ruts created by Campbell's earlier, successful effort and the intermittent rain.

The Stutz Black Hawk was towed to the starting line at the south end of the course. Lockhart hit the accelerator and started to pick up speed. He was going about 190 mph when the rain intensified. Suddenly unable to see as the fog obscured his vision, Lockhart ran into some soft sand and lost control. The car headed straight for the ocean.

"A huge fountain of water was thrown 100 feet high; the car, almost too swift to see, leapt high above the waves, crashed in an upflung cloud of spray and leaped again 20 feet above the water. It turned a complete double somersault, and then thundered into the surf, almost buried from sight," Day reported.

Lockhart was pinned inside. The upright Black Hawk was buried in sand up to the white tops of the tires. Every time a wave crested, Lockhart was submerged. A local man, Gil Farrell, was credited with saving Lockhart's life by telling him when to hold his breath beneath an onrushing wave. Farrell later raced on the beach and, ironically, drowned in a creek.

Eventually, dozens of onlookers were able to link hands and drag the car onto the beach. An-

5259

Frank Lockhart poses with a crowd before starting on his fatal attempt to set a new land-speed record in 1928. Motorsports Images & Archives Photo

other report said a truck was involved. Lockhart survived with three torn tendons in his wrist. He also vowed to come back and wrest the title from whoever held it.

Ray Keech was next in line. He brought the Triplex, a monster car with three airplane engines under its massive hood. The engines had been used during World War I and turned out an estimated 1,125 hp. Owned by Jim White from Philadelphia, the car contained 36 cylinders of "roaring horsepower" and was probably the largest race car ever driven. Essentially a rolling tank that weighed more than five tons and came equipped with six wheels—only four of which ever touched the ground at

one time—the Triplex was 5,000 cubic inches of "roaring, smoking, vibrating race car." Keech had his own description of it: "crude, bulky and hard to steer."

The Triplex had never been tested before and was built from spare parts drawn from boats and airplanes. It had no reverse gear, which should have disqualified it based on the rules of the day, but some last-second crude alterations allowed it to go backwards at about a half-mile an hour. That was deemed sufficient to gain approval from the AAA.

The car hit 201 mph before an engine valve broke and shot superheated radiator fluid into the driver's face. Temporarily blinded, Keech stuck his head out the window and hung on before managing to halt the car safely two miles later. That was a good thing. Exhaust fumes blowing into his face almost asphyxiated him. An engine fire added a few burns to his injuries. To add a final insult, he did not top Campbell's time.

The contest ended with Campbell getting ready to make one more try, but having to desist because too many spectators had overrun the course. Not that it mattered. The Scotsman had set a world record and outraced two American competitors in their own country. Campbell was named an honorary American Police Constable, visited President Calvin Coolidge in the White House and went home to great acclaim.

His place on top of the record book did not last long.

Keech, who would die in 1929 in a Pennsylvania race shortly after winning the Indianapolis 500, returned to Daytona April 22, 1928 with the Triplex and averaged 207.552 mph to seize the speed crown again.

On April 25, Lockhart quickly tried to match him. In his first two practice runs, he actually posted records in the American two-to-three-liter class. He then aimed at Keech's world record.

Still broke, he elected not to change tires for his return run. Campbell had advised him to replace all four tires after each sprint down the beach. Lockhart didn't have the money for that and decided to risk it. That was a fatal mistake. At the end of his third run, a jagged clam shell pierced the Black Hawk's right rear tire, according to historian Tuthill. Lockhart did not realize it. Midway through his fourth run, the damaged tire burst, his Stutz went into an uncontrolled spin, somersaulted three times and came to rest upside down in a heap of metal. Lockhart was thrown more than 50 feet from his demolished car and killed instantly.

Daytona Beach residents created a fund to ship the body of the penniless driver back to his home in California. His widow absconded with the money, according to the book *Daytona: The Quest for Speed* by reporter Tom Tucker and photographer Jim Tiller. A second collection finally raised enough to pay for sending Lockhart back to California for burial five months after his accident. His mother couldn't help with the costs. Prior to his final race, she had appealed to her son for $10. Poignantly, he had wired her back: "I have the world by the horns. You'll never have to push a needle again. I'll never have to work anymore."

Undaunted by Lockhart's death or loss of his own speed record, Segrave came back to Daytona Beach on March 11, 1929 with a Napier Golden Arrow and easily eclipsed Keech's mark, clocking in at 231.44 mph. His elongated car, painted gold, featured a gunsight mounted on the hood to help the driver aim down the course. Designed with a chiseled, aerodynamic front end, the Golden Arrow was powered by a 12-cylinder airplane engine with the cylinders arranged in three banks of four.

Keech was invited to respond in the Triplex, but he refused, insisting he was too busy building his next entry for the Indianapolis 500, and that he didn't trust the car. "There's not enough money to get me back in that hot seat," he announced.

Car owner White, who patriotically wanted

SPEED RECORDS

The Federation International de L'Automobile (FIA) in Paris became the accrediting body for all motorsports records in the early part of the 20th century. In the United States, the American Automobile Association handled that task until the mid-1950s. For many years, the two operated separately before finally reaching an agreement in 1927. Major H.O.D. Segrave was the catalyst for the dÈtente. He insisted that his attempt that year to set the speed record must be acceptable to both groups.

Since Segrave was making his run on American soil, it was to the AAA's advantage to be sure any record was recognized worldwide.

Previous record runs by Bob Burman, Ralph DePalma, Tommy Milton and Jimmy Murphy, however, do not show up on official records.

The dry, smooth lake beds in Utah and Nevada eventually replaced Daytona Beach as the sites for drivers looking to go faster than anyone has before. Jet engines were inserted under hoods until the cars looked more like horizontal rockets than anything Henry Ford imagined coming off an assembly line.

The golden age of speed racing took place on Daytona's hard sand and ended with Sir Malcolm Campbell's record run in 1935. He broke the 300-mph barrier soon after in Utah, but the quest for the record became sporadic.

Between 1936 and 1982, only a few drivers bothered to try to break the record. Then, in 1983, Richard Noble hit a record 633.46 mph during a run across open spaces in Nevada. His car was powered by a Rolls Royce engine, the same company that produced Malcolm Campbell's 1935 Bluebird engine.

That record held for 14 years until RAF Captain Andy Green steered a 10-ton roadster—aptly named Trust and equipped with two Rolls-Royce jet engines—to the new record of 763 mph in October 1997. Green broke the sound barrier along with the speed record.

He was on the Black Rock Desert in Nevada at the time.

These days, there's no racing along the Daytona Beach shoreline anymore, except by an occasional visitor who tops the posted 10-mph limit and by the antique cars that flock to Ormond Beach, "the Birthplace of Speed," to put on exhibitions every November.

Instead, there are only white balls of foam, racing on at the whim of the wind, and fragile as any record pursued by a group of drivers who lived—and occasionally died—for a moment of glory as the fastest human on four wheels.

Here are the internationally recognized land speed record times and the men who achieved them.

Year	Driver	Miles Per Hour
1898	Gaston de Chasseloup–Laubat Acheres, France	39.24
1904	Louis Rigolly Ostend, Belgium	103.56
1906	Fred Marriott Daytona Beach	127.57
1922	Kebelem Lee Guiness Brooklands, England	129.17
1925	Malcolm Campbell Pendine, Wales	146.16
1925	Malcolm Campbell Pendine, Wales	150.86
1927	Henry Segrave Daytona Beach	203.79
1928	Malcolm Campbell Daytona Beach	206.95
1928	Ray Keech Daytona Beach	207.55
1929	Henry Segrave Daytona Beach	231.44
1931	Malcolm Campbell Daytona Beach	246.09
1935	Malcolm Campbell Daytona Beach	276.82
1935	Malcolm Campbell Bonneville, Utah	301.13
1937	George Eyston Bonneville, Utah	312.00
1983	Richard Noble Black Rock Desert, Nevada	633.46
1997	Andy Green Black Rock Desert, Nevada	763.00

to recapture a record held by foreigners but set on American soil, then turned to Lee Bible, an otherwise-unknown local resident who ran a Daytona Beach garage. Bible called the chance to drive the car "a golden opportunity" and the key to his success. He then made several practice runs to demonstrate he could control the huge vehicle.

There is a photo of Bible seated in the massive car along the shoreline on March 12, 1929. He's wearing a small helmet with goggles up, his left arm waving a greeting to the crowd. His wife, Anna, who owned a Main Street newsstand, and their daughter, Grace, were in the stands that day to watch him.

Around 3 p.m., Bible made another rapid trip down the beach and handled the "snorting monster" with little apparent problem.

Bible then started north and passed through

the measured mile at about 200 mph, following a "30-foot-long wake of black smoke and sand." Suddenly, inexplicably, the huge car swerved to the west and headed for the crowded dunes.

Pathe News cameraman Charles Traub had tried to move closer to get a better picture. He only saw the Triplex bearing down on him. Apparently panicking, he sprinted across the sand and ended up directly in front of the roaring vehicle, according to Neely.

"The big car struck the cameraman squarely, cleaving his body," the *News-Journal* reported in its March 13 edition. "In a split second, the mighty machine crashed into the dunes about 100 feet from the timing trap, showering the air with sand and smoke. The Triplex rolled, bounding over and over until it came up against the dunes, at least 200 feet further north." Traub was dismembered. Bible was thrown at least 100 feet from the demolished car.

Rushed to the hospital by ambulance, Bible died en route. His death prompted owner White to quit racing. "It was a very regrettable thing," he said. "I have no further ambition."

Segrave, too, was still in town and badly shaken by the accident. He announced that he would forego racing on dry land and try to set his next record on water. He headed for the nearby Halifax

The famed Bluebird, driven by Malcolm Campbell, drew a crowd en route to its record run in 1935. Speed racing in Daytona Beach ended that year, giving way to stock cars and motorcycles.
Motorsports Images & Archives Photo

River to demonstrate his white boat he had named *Miss England*. The craft was particularly buoyant, an effect achieved by filling the hull with thousands of ping-pong balls. Segrave eventually became the only man to date to hold speed records on land and water. However, in 1930, he died in his native country when *Miss England* crashed during another attempt to break the water-speed record.

Campbell would not back away. He felt that Segrave's death left him as the only driver available still capable of cracking the 240-mph barrier. Described as "lean and hard with an almost imperturbable manner," he would outlive all of his competitors, dying after an operation for glaucoma in 1948. Weakening eyesight had forced him to retire from racing two years earlier.

"I never grew up," Campbell once told reporters, insisting he viewed life as "a grand adventure." He would have been a "pirate if he had lived in the right age," he informed Thomas Wisdom of the *London Daily Herald* in 1933.

Wisdom then noted that Campbell "is superstitious, although he pretends not to be. He dislikes the number 13, does not regard Friday as a good day for racing and refuses to walk under ladders."

The reporter also recorded that Campbell had little success in his effort to achieve any speed records until he went to Daytona Beach. "He says that Daytona is 'his' course," the morning editor wrote.

The community reciprocated the warm feelings. Every Campbell visit became a social happening with celebrations and parties. He recognized

his hosts' enthusiasm by having the flags of the United States and Great Britain painted side by side on the hood of each Bluebird.

He also kept going faster. In February 1931, Campbell ratcheted up the record speed to 245.73 mph. His Bluebird featured a Napier engine with an extra boost to achieve 1,350 hp.

In 1932, having been knighted by King George IV, Campbell returned to shatter his own standard, clocking in at 253.97 mph. That was 17 mph faster than the aviation speed record set earlier that year.

He also stunned the racing world by insisting the 300 mph mark would fall next. He did not say where the event would take place. Increasingly, Campbell was becoming convinced that a new track had to be found.

"The speed factor alone in record-breaking had now become quite dangerous enough without the anxiety of uncertain surfaces, and pounding surf and dangerous soft sand dunes flanking the narrow strip," biographer Hough said.

Campbell tried to pinpoint sites in Africa and in England with no success. When the Daytona Chamber of Commerce invited him back in December 1933, he reluctantly accepted.

"One hundred thousand dollars is the price Sir Malcolm Campbell will pay for the privilege of risking his neck on the wave-packed sands of Daytona Beach," wrote UPS reporter Henry McLemore, who came to Florida to witness the attempt. "The $100,000 represents the cost of outfitting the 1933 venture, and it will come out of his own pocket, too. Sir Malcolm has no backers; he does not make his runs as an advertising stint for any firm. When the mighty Bluebird roars down the beach, it roars solely for the honor of Sir Malcolm and the Union Jack."

Historian Tuthill was on the scene and recorded his impressions. He was particularly taken by the tires, which he described as "perfectly smooth, a paper-thin coating of rubber holding together 18 plies of silk and cotton cord. They cost $1,800 each and had a life of seven minutes."

They got a workout as Campbell had to fight to control his car. The sand looks and feels hard, but the surface is uneven with tiny imperfections that can force a car off line. At the speed Campbell was going, he needed all his strength to stay on course. Still, in his latest Bluebird, Campbell managed to hit 328 mph at one point, but the friction created by the sand and the undulating surface left the average at "only" 273.5 mph. That was a record, but well below the predicted 300-mph level.

"The huge numbers to my left, set at each mile post, jump into my vision," Campbell wrote after the run. "My foot is hard on the accelerator. I see, as a thing detached, the yellow-and-black rectangular marker above the start of the mile. I press my foot down harder. I wait ages, it seems. Time does not fly; it creeps. At last, there is another rectangular yellow-and-black marker overhead. I find myself breathing again, as though I had not before. I have finished my record run. It has taken me seconds, just over 12, but it seems like ages."

For the next two years, Campbell worked on the car, trying to find every ounce of speed. He was able to conjure up a 2,700-hp burst from the 2,227-cubic-inch V-12 engine, which only provided a lifespan of three minutes. "At peak speed," Tuthill noted, "he could pull a lever in the cockpit which snapped shut the four-inch opening across the nose (there to improve air flow and downforce) and gain an additional 12 miles per hour."

Finally, in January 1935, Campbell, mechanic Leo Villa and the Bluebird arrived in Daytona Beach for what would turn out to be the last time. Bad weather seemed to have cancelled the planned run on March 7, and most spectators left early. However, late in the afternoon, Campbell decided conditions were optimal.

Among those watching him in the meager crowd that day was William Henry Getty France, a race car driver and mechanic originally from Virginia. Years later, France would buy the Bluebird that sped by him that cloudy afternoon.

"I wound up owning the car I came to watch run down those sands here all those years ago," France mused decades later. "Sometimes life works out like that."

The big car, weighing five tons, swayed as it careened down the sand, shredding its Dunlop tires. The slightest imperfection in the sand caused the car to slip sideways, but Campbell still managed to top 330 miles per hour on his third run.

Tuthill was in the grandstand as the car roared past. "First, a black dot appeared far up the beach and quickly took shape as it approached in utter silence," he wrote. "The Bluebird was outrunning its exhaust noise. A blue flame, and a sudden blast like thunder, and it was gone. After the shock wave, all heads turned. Now the car was out of sight in the other direction, obscured by whirling sand. We did see a big blue ball that hung in midair for a second then disappeared. That ear-shattering blast and the eerie ball of flame when Campbell cut the throttle are the only memories I have as an eyewitness of the fastest run ever made on the world-famous measured mile."

Malcolm Campbell owned 16 different Bluebirds, each designed for maximum speed. This one tested the beach and the limits of speed in 1931. Motorsports Images & Archives Photo

Campbell couldn't match his speed on the second try. Two bumps in the sand once again shredded tires. He tried two more times, but topped out at an average of 276.82 mph. That was another record, but not the 300 mph that Campbell craved.

By the end of the day, he was convinced the beach could never handle higher speeds. Unwilling to give up his chase for 300 mph, Campbell moved to the Bonneville Salt Flats on a one-mile course. There, he hit an average of 305 mph on his first run. He turned around and headed back. His oil line cracked en route, "spraying the windshield and cockpit with smoke and fumes. Campbell was nearly unconscious when he came to a stop at the other end of the salt flats." His average run, however, came to 301 mph.

The engines that powered his Bluebirds were later installed in the fighters that would win the Battle of Britain in World War II. "The test bench for those remarkable engines was Sir Malcolm Campbell's Bluebird, and the proving ground was 17 miles of Daytona Beach straightaway," Tuthill proudly noted. (Tucker and Tiller labeled that claim "a good story.")

Nevertheless, 1935 proved to be Campbell's last visit to Daytona Beach, which he called his second home. When he left, city leaders realized he took the tourist industry with him. Already in the middle of a depression, they could only envision a dark economic future no longer brightened by the blue flame from the back of a speeding car.

c h a p t e r f i v e

ON THE BEACH

Sir Malcolm Campbell came to Daytona Beach and paid for everything from his own pocket. Other racers, not as wealthy, needed subsidies. Daytona Beach officials chipped in as much as $30,000 to convince renowned drivers like Segrave and Don to drive on the famous beach. As a marketing ploy to keep the Daytona Beach name in the public eye, it was successful but had one significant limitation. When drivers realized that the beach was not smooth enough to handle ever-increasing speeds, they no longer were interested in any offers.

Not sure what to do, city officials debated several suggestions, including hosting races on the beach. It was not a new idea. Four years earlier, B. Thornton, secretary and public relations director of the Daytona Beach Speedway Association, tried to start races on the beach. An undated newspaper clipping quotes Thornton as saying he went to Indianapolis to talk to organizers there and soon realized how much money was needed to do the job properly. Lacking the funds, he dropped the concept.

In addition, the beach already hosted barrel races, beginning in the early 1920s as benefits for various charities. "Souped up and chopped down roadsters," author Fielden called them, sprinted around tight ovals created by barrels. Drivers were paid little; instead any income went for Christmas baskets and the like. No one expected such events would capture headlines either, although one 100-miler in 1930 included 21 cars and, according to a published report, was broadcast by Henry Vedder of A.B.C.

Bill France (No. 10) was so successful and popular as a driver that fans prevented a rival promoter from banning him from racing. **Motorsports Images & Archives Photo**

Baker "on his program." It was run by the Speedway Association, which is otherwise unidentified, as a benefit for the Elks Club. Barney Sullivan was listed as the promoter, but said he wouldn't do any more because of gatecrashers.

There had also been some sports festivals that featured racing. Sponsored by the Florida Auto Racing Association, one event in 1922 was highlighted by an exhibit by Sig Haugdahl, who set an unofficial speed record earlier in the year. Also, famed female dirt-track driver, Zenita Neville, became the first woman to drive in open competition against men, according to a newspaper report.

Given that kind of history in motorsports, City Council members figured that races remained the best option for Daytona's future. The barrels were eliminated. Instead the drivers would compete on the sand for purses not designated for charity.

Who actually oversaw the first official race is unclear. In a letter written in 1974, former city attorney Millard Conklin reported he "conceived, planned and staged" the initial event on what was called the Beach-Road Facility. Wanting the course to be as authentic as possible, he hired former driver Haugdahl

Lockhart

Wreck of the Stutz Black Hawk
Photo by LESESNE

When Frank Lockhart (arrow) crashed during his attempt to set a land-speed record in 1928, he had to be rescued by local residents. A year later, he was killed in a second try at the record. **Motorsports Images & Archives Photo**

Johnny Rutherford (No. 29) tries to navigate the deep ruts of the north turn of the Beach-Road Course in 1936. His Auburn boattail eventually got bogged down. So did every other car competing that day. Motorsports Images & Archives Photo

to design it. Historian Fielden, however, said city officials (of which Conklin was one) contacted Haugdahl "to discuss the idea of presenting some sort of speed contest."

Regardless of who gets the credit, Haugdahl was the perfect choice to set up the first race. Largely retired from racing by then, the diminutive Norwegian had been the first man to record an unofficial three-minute mile. Haugdahl, whose interest was focused on Midgets and not bigger cars, owned a gas station and built his own vehicles. He had worked with Lockhart and the ill-fated Black Hawk, and then with Segrave on his *Miss England*. He rode as a mechanic with Segrave in the Miss America VIII matches held on the water in 1929 and helped install the Napier engines in the speedboat.

Haugdahl also became well known for his own racing prowess between the early 1920s to the mid-1930s, winning seven consecutive Midwest dirt-track titles. Bill France, the eventual founder of NASCAR, knew him, too. The two men had already talked about creating some kind of track that incorporated the beach and the paved road—now straight, but then featuring an s-curve—running alongside it. The design would be inexpensive and easy to set up. Participating cars had to be "stock," matching up with manufacturers' specifications.

When the AAA came on board in January 1936 as the sanctioning body, the race was set for March. Not everyone was thrilled with the plan. Weaned on media-heavy visits by international drivers chasing the highly prized land-speed record,

SPONSORSHIP

When the first cars rolled down the beach in the early part of the 1900s, the drivers were employees of car manufacturers, who participated in the races in an effort to increase recognition for their products. Sir Malcolm Campbell, who was wealthy enough to pay his own expenses, was an exception.

Producers of automotive products got into the act after the Indianapolis Speedway opened in 1909. The first Indianapolis 500 was held two years later and quickly developed a reputation as the most prestigious race in motorsports. Companies would tout their connection to the winner, including the brand of tires, motor oil, gasoline and the like. At one time, both companies provided tires to drivers competing in the Indianapolis 500, Goodyear Tire & Rubber Co. and Firestone Rubber Co., for example, would prepare advertisements promoting the competitors using their tires and would publish an ad touting the winning driver immediately after the race ended. Goodyear these days focuses solely on stock-car racing.

Prior to the beach races, a variety of companies were eager sponsors of racing and cars. Gilmore Oil and Riverside Tires, a division of Montgomery Ward, were among the most active. In addition, based on archival photographs, many drivers could count on some local support and would paint the name of the company on their cars. C.D. "Smokey" Purser, for example, painted the name of his restaurant on the driver's side of his car.

In the early years of racing, the cost to the sponsor may have been nothing more than a sample of a product. Prices shot up in recent years as the fan base widened.

The August 5, 1999, issue of *NASCAR Winston Cup Scene* magazine reported that a company may spend $8 million to support a race team and an equal amount for promotions and for entertaining clients.

By 2003, that tab may have doubled.

Not every business can ante up that kind of money. Companies that have maintained long-term car sponsorships include Budweiser, Miller, Coors, Tide, Valvoline, CITGO, Texaco/Havoline and GM Goodwrench. Valvoline made history in 2000 by buying part of the No. 10 team owned by MBV Motorsports.

Some of the long-term sponsors who have backed away from sponsorship in recent years include STP, Skoal, Quaker State, Kodiak and McDonald's. CITGO dropped out at the end of 2003.

The average lifespan of a NASCAR NEXTEL Cup sponsorship is four to six years, according to marketing guru Tom Cotter. "It is very often a change in management where a new company is acquired or merged, or a new vice president of marketing takes over," he added. "People in these positions don't like to ride on the coattail of their predecessors."

The emphasis has shifted over the years too. "It used to be a real benefit for anybody just to put their name on the track, go around in circles and get on TV. But, companies [now] are in it for one reason—business to business. They want to find new customers through auto racing," explained Dave Wells, commercial director for Precision Preparation Inc., which started in the CART Series and off-road racing before moving into NASCAR in 2000.

The impact of sponsorship often reaches beyond actual sales.

Fans associate the driver and the sponsor. Studies published by the *SportsBusiness Journal* have found that racing fans are extremely loyal to their chosen driver and the products that driver is associated with.

"NASCAR fans realize that if sponsors weren't involved in the sport, then the sport wouldn't be where it is today," explained Dean Kessel, manager of sports marketing for Lowe's, once sponsor of the No. 48 Chevrolet. "So, they reward those sponsors by a conscious effort of going into your store or buying your product."

Companies often focus their marketing strategies around racing. "Entertainment and hospitality have become the driving force behind [marketing] programs, creating huge hospitality villages at every NASCAR Winston Cup track," said *NASCAR Winston Cup Scene*'s Jeff Owens in 2002. "Although numerous fans are invited through sweepstakes promotions and sponsor connections, it is corporate executives who are the focus of the program."

The marketing push has enhanced the quality of racing and technology. Winning drivers help boost sales. So, companies pushed for more technologically advanced vehicles that are also safer. "All of them want to win, and they don't care how pretty or ugly the [driver] is if he can get the job done," said veteran car owner Robert Yates.

Sponsors have helped reduce ancillary problems. Companies do not want drivers with background problems representing them. "In NASCAR Winston Cup racing today," Owens wrote in 2002, "image is everything." Not only does the driver have to look good and speak well, "he has to have an image that presents his sponsor in a positive light."

Steve Saunders, field marketing manager for Coors, said, "Your driver needs to match what you are doing. There are some who are just terrific matches. The guy bleeds what he's sponsored by, but it's not always easy to find the right fit."

As a result of the corporate scrutiny, few drivers in modern times have been arrested or suffered the kinds of public embarrassment associated with other sports.

Drivers, in turn, have mostly avoided the kinds of confrontations and comments likely to create unrest. While that approach has led to complaints that drivers are almost robotic in their responses, the focus inherently becomes the races themselves and not the extraneous activities away from the track.

Sponsors will become even more important in the future. "If you won every race," said car owner Tim Beverly, "you still couldn't afford to run a race team without a sponsor."

several political leaders wanted an attraction more substantial and prestigious than a bunch of local racers sprinting up and down "The World's Most Famous Beach."

The local chamber also provided "less than enthusiastic support," according to Tom Neff, writing in *Auto Racing Memories*.

In addition, several church groups objected. A local church organization unanimously "decried the action of the instigators and promoters of the race as ungodly, and also as undesirable by most of our best citizens and tourists and as a stigma on the highest reputation of our community." Another church complained about the Sunday race date.

On the other hand, beach racing still held a lot of attraction. Besides, in the midst of the Depression, no one could think of a better idea to draw tourists. Racing was not expected to be big business, only a winter diversion that would garner some headlines for tiny Daytona Beach.

Haugdahl had never designed a track before. Neither had France.

France was only a race-car driver who owned a local gas station. A big man, standing about six foot five, France had been born in Virginia in 1909. Mechanically inclined, he built a Model-T for racing as a teenager and tried it out on local tracks in nearby Maryland. He played basketball, worked at a bank and followed the reports of speed records falling on the beach in Daytona.

By 1927, he found a job working as a battery and electric system repairman for a Washington service-station chain, then moved to a local Ford dealership as a front-end specialist.

Whenever possible, he went racing in the family car. "It was hard to keep a straight face when his (father) went down to the tire dealer to complain about his tires wearing out so fast on his Model T," his son, Bill Jr., recalled years later.

The economy was bad in the 1930s. The

country had begun to slide into the Depression in 1929 and would not recover until midway through World War II. Like many Americans, France thought he could find economic security someplace else. The South seemed inviting. So France and his wife, Anne, a former nurse, bought a small trailer, hooked it to the back of their Ford, piled their young son and the family belongings inside, and headed toward the Sunshine State. Their intended destination was Miami.

France had $75 in his bank account, $25 in his pocket and a set of tools. When the family reached Daytona Beach, he stopped the car to check out the famous beach. Despite later reports that his car had broken down, forcing him to stay, France was actually lured to the area by previous newspaper accounts about racing. If the car had a problem, he pointed out, he could have fixed it.

"We drove across the Ormond Bridge and out on the beach," France recalled in the 1970s. Ironically, that route took him past the Hotel Ormond, the original home of racing. "The tide was out, and I remember looking down the beach and seeing the tide for the first time. It was a beautiful fall day, and there wasn't a soul on the beach." They drove south to the Main Street Pier. "We changed into our swimming trunks in the trailer and went swimming," he said.

The idyllic stopover ended any thoughts of continuing their drive. "I just liked Daytona, and we decided it was where we wanted to be," France said. After a few days of rest with a friend in New Smyrna Beach, a small community to the south of Daytona, France found a job as a mechanic at a local Pontiac, Buick, Cadillac dealership called the Daytona Motor Co. In his spare time, he raced on dirt tracks throughout the south in a car nicknamed the Blitzkreik Special.

He also made a few rapid trips up and down the shoreline. "If you are interested in racing at all, you just don't live at the beach without using it," France explained.

Shortly after watching the Bluebird fly down the sand, France bought his own gas station. A replica of the small station is now set up in DAYTONA USA, not far from the Bluebird.

"Business wasn't good at first," France recalled, "so I had plenty of time to fish and race." As a result, the young mechanic became familiar with other competitors, including Haugdahl.

The two men were delighted when their proposal for a beach race finally passed city council. They immediately set up the course. It would feature 1.6 miles of beach driving and an equal distance on the narrow blacktop road known as A1A. The north turn almost touched the start of the old Measured Mile. The South Turn was on land owned by a local resident, William McIntyre, and selected because of the easy access to the dunes. Wooden bleachers were erected on both turns.

The city council coughed up $5,000 as the purse for a "strictly stock automobile" race. The high-priced rocket ships now belonged to history. Daytona Beach was going to aim at a slower, less-

In 1935, Malcolm Campbell rode this Bluebird to his last world speed record to be set on the sand at Daytona Beach—more than 278 mph. The raised air flaps indicate the car is on its cool-down portion of the run. Motorsports Images & Archives Photo

Sig Haugdahl set a land-speed record in 1922, then, 14 years later, joined with Bill France to promote the first stock car race on the beach in Daytona. **Motorsports Images & Archives Photo**

elite market, eventually drawing competitors who typically got their training by outrunning revenuers in the southern backwoods.

The race was scheduled for 250 miles and was divided into four classes based on sticker price: up to $665, $666–$900, $901–$1,300; more than $1,301. Any car that averaged more than three mph above its qualifying speed would automatically be booted out.

Cars had to be 1935 or 1936 models, carry one spare tire and no bumpers. Windshields had to be upright. Doors must be anchored shut and hoods strapped down. Foreign cars were barred initially. And there was only room for 36 cars. That last restriction did not come into play. Only 27 cars showed up for the race, although 55 drivers originally submitted entry forms.

To the joy of city officials, who were anxiously counting every penny, the first race attracted the elite in motorsports, their eyes riveted on the big purse. Jim Malone, who was also a city official and pressed reluctantly into promoting the race, declined to pay any appearance fees, although he did spring for publicity photos of young women in bathing suits waving flags and posing with cars.

While a few stars chose not to bring their cars to Daytona Beach, many of the top drivers did come, reviving memories of the sandfest from the early 1900s. Heading the field was former Indianapolis 500 winner Bill Cummings. Sam and Miles Collier, who would later promote sports-car events at Sebring and Watkins Glen, entered. So did dirt-track champions Bob Sall, George "Doc" Mackenzie and Ben Shaw. Midget racing champ Bill Schindler showed up along with English star Major A.T.G. "Goldie" Gardner. Ten of the drivers were from Florida. A variety of cars were in that first grid, including19 V-8 Fords; two Auburns; two Willys, which were the slowest entrants; and one each from Chevrolet, Dodge, Zephyr and Oldsmobile.

France brought his 1935 Ford and served as a mechanic on Milt Marion's Ford. In a letter written in 1984, France said Marion's car was painted blue, and his was black. He couldn't recall the color of the interiors.

He was ready to race. "I had an advantage over a lot of them," France said. "I had been there a couple of years, and I knew how to drive in the sand."

Both men also enjoyed some outside help. Permatex became one of the first companies to sponsor a car by backing Marion. The company provided a gasket solution. France removed several gaskets, so the driver could use the product. Ucal Cunningham, a Daytona gasoline distributor, outfitted France with fuel and tires. Previously, sponsorships typically had been limited to a handful of the cars competing in the Indianapolis 500.

A variety of reporters showed up, too, drawn by the unusual track conditions as well as by Daytona's racing history. McLemore, who had been on hand to watch the Bluebird set records, came back to report on the stock car race.

Cummings qualified first at 70.39 mph. Like the other drivers, he had to qualify while the tide washed the course, so there would be time to hold the race during low tide. Qualifying required five days to complete.

At 1 p.m., drivers gathered at the starting line. Meanwhile, Haugdahl was engaged in a totally different venue. Several political opponents of beach racing ran off with the purse and tickets. Gathering an army of reporters, Haugdahl stormed City Hall and found the missing money.

"The tickets showed up later after several thousand people got in free," he said. "We really didn't care at that point. As long as we had the prize money, we were going to have a race."

The stands were full. An estimated 20,000 people attended the event, although few actually paid. There was no way to prevent people from driving down A1A and walking across the road to sit on the dunes. Ticket sellers located along the course had little success selling tickets to anyone already watching the race. Advanced ticket sales did total about $6,000, covering the purse but not expenses. Local reporter Bob Hunter said any deficit would be "charged to promotions."

The cars lined up an hour before low tide, four or five abreast. Some had numbers; others merely had names painted on the drivers' side doors. Based on the program, numbers were apparently assigned in order as each entry came in, not on qualifying times. The numbers ran sequentially in the program listings.

"We didn't know until qualifying time if the beach was going to be smooth or rough," France said. He also had to worry about an east wind, which could hurry the tide back in.

The slowest cars were sent off first, with the pole winner going off last, more than 30 minutes later. There were no standards, no inspections or controls on tires. Any driver who had a car and was willing to show up was allowed to compete. They rode on the original equipment tires that the cars came with.

A truck equipped with a public address system drove up and down the beach warning spectators to stay off the course.

Cummings, who started 30 minutes and 40 seconds behind the lead cars, easily caught up with the earlier competitors, but didn't survive long. His Auburn quickly clogged with sand and was fin-

ished after 16 laps. Jack Rutherfurd, a famed car and boat racer, was forced to quit after 26 laps. MacKenzie was one of the first out as a result of "stuffing" his Ford into a sand dune.

"The big, heavy cars had a disadvantage," France said. Sinking lower into the beach, they sucked sand into the engines and rapidly expired. The lighter cars, like his Ford, however, ran higher and plowed through the beach. Each lap, however, deepened the ruts. Photographs show canyon-like grooves that rocked cars from side to side and made every turn hazardous. If a car went too slowly into the turn, it got stuck and had to be pulled out. Marion, driving the car France prepared, was towed on five occasions, then caught up on the long straightaways. Too fast in a turn, and a car flipped over. The race dragged on as tow trucks kept busy. Every car was towed at least twice.

New Yorker Bill Lawrence "got out of his car when it was stuck in the North Turn, and with a small camera devoted himself to taking pictures." reporter Hunter wrote.

The *Miami Tribune* melodramatically called the race a "duel with death."

Englishman "Goldie" Gardner was more polite. He quit after 45 laps and described it as "an obstacle course."

"The punishment was so severe that most of the cars that got beyond the halfway mark had front wheels severely out of line," Hunter noted.

UP's McLemore claimed the South Turn had become a "hog wallow. It was not a road. Just a mess of holes that a horse would have trouble getting through."

To make matters worse, all the towing and turning left officials completely bewildered. No one knew who was leading the race. To compound the confusion, harkening back to the chaos of 1906, the slow-moving event meant the tide had time to start rolling back in. Pushed by a stronger-than-expected east wind, the Atlantic began pouring onto the beach. Drivers found themselves forced to steer through the surf, which began softening the sand. Hundreds of spectators scrambled into the cars and fled down the beach to exit ramps, trying to avoid being stranded along the dunes and steering clear of the racers. At one point, the dry portion of the course was only 15 feet wide. There were no grooves anyway. At low tide, cars were often five or six abreast.

After more than four hours on the course, a handful of race cars chugged into the deep North Turn ruts and got stuck there. Behind them, the tide grew ominously closer. Spectators were now clamoring to escape. More drivers were headed for the North Turn. Harried AAA officials made the only possible decision—they called the race after 241 miles and declared a winner.

"Moon-faced" Milt Marion, as the *Florida Times Union* labeled him, took home the $1,700 top prize. A Canadian dirt-track champion, he had started 20th.

"How they figured out who won the race, I don't know," France said. "They said Marion won,

This is the entry list for the first beach race. Many of these drivers were famous and drawn to Daytona by a hefty purse. Motorsports Images & Archives Photo

Ben Shaw was second and Tommy Elmore was third, but no one really knew. There was too much confusion." France was awarded fifth.

The combination of lost tickets and the big purse caused a financial shortfall. The city lost $22,000 and saw no reason to plan a second event.

Beach racing—and racing in general in Daytona Beach—looked to have finally ended after 33 years.

chapter six

1936-38

While City Hall bemoaned its losses, France and Haugdahl began to fish around for another funding source. Neither of them had enough money to underwrite a 1937 race or guarantee the purse. The local Daytona Elks Club finally put up the cash, but officials there insisted they were not going to spend much money. They didn't. As a result, the $100 prize wasn't remotely close to the 1936 jackpot, but at least the race was on.

The promoters shifted the date to Labor Day, a choice that would reverberate in motorsports history. When NASCAR's first superspeedway, Darlington Raceway, opened in 1950, its inaugural event was held coincidently on the same holiday weekend. As an aside, the man who built that historic track, Harold Brasington, competed on the beach in 1938 and finished fourth.

The new date and underwriter for the 1937 event could not affect the quality of racing. However, the tide wasn't going to disappear. The ruts had to. Otherwise, the race would deteriorate again along with the course. No one wanted to see tow trucks spending more time on the beach than the race cars.

The answer came from another city-sponsored event. Simply because the 1936 race lost money didn't mean that city officials had lost their taste or enthusiasm for motorsports.

They turned to motorcycles. Conceivably, the lighter bikes would be able to negotiate the turns without making a shambles of the race course.

Ironically, prior to 1930, motorcycle racing in America was pretty much in a state of shambles itself, reported Don Emde in his book, *The Daytona 200: The History of America's Premier Motorcycle Race.*

OPPOSITE: **In 1936, Bill France helped set up the race course on the beach and promote the first stock car race in Daytona. Motorsports Images & Archives Photo**

The onrushing tide forced an end to the first beach race in 1936 after more than four hours of competition. Motorsports Images & Archives Photo

Motorcycle racing had been popular entertainment until 1925. The country's first 300-mile race had been run on a 3.22-mile course in Savannah, Georgia, since 1913. Unfortunately, a rash of deaths and injuries at motorcycle events led to the banning of exotic machinery, which had little in common with their street counterparts. Coupled with the Depression, interest in two-wheel competition fell off at both the spectator and manufacturer levels.

In 1932, four veteran motorcycle enthusiasts— John Balmer, Walt Cunningham, George Cleary and Jim Flowers—decided to promote a major motorcycle event in the Southeast. With the assistance of several motorcycle dealers, they formed the Southeastern Motorcycle Dealers Association and revived the Savannah Cup races as a 200-mile event. The race utilized the American Motorcycle Association's Class "C" rules, which were basically street motorcycles with headlights and mufflers removed.

The race was held in 1932 and 1933 in Savannah. Both races lost money, with the initial event attracting only 13 entries—although a rider on the sidelines was persuaded to start to avoid the "un-

lucky" number 13. The following year, 23 riders participated, and the event generated some national interest. The races then moved to Camp Foster in Jacksonville, Florida for 1934 and 1935, where they were more successful. The field grew to 48 and then 68 riders, spectator numbers increased, and the races generated plenty of attention, both nationally and in Canada. With Camp Foster unable to accommodate the growing crowds, the event moved back to its original site in Savannah for 1936, where 73 riders competed.

That's where Daytona Beach stepped in. The prospect of racing in Florida during the winter offered a strong incentive, and the group accepted the city's offer to use Daytona Beach for the 1937 event. The Daytona 200 had found itself a permanent home.

The race was set for January 24, 1937. The promoters were well aware of the problems the stock car drivers had run into the year before. To prevent the turns from breaking up, they brought several dozen truckloads of marl, which the dictionary defines as "a loose or crumbling earthy deposit (as of sand, silt, or clay) that contains a substantial amount of calcium carbonate and is used especially as a fertilizer for soils deficient in lime." It has another distinction: it turns rock hard when packed and dry. Bill France and his drivers watched the results very carefully.

What they saw had to please them. A field of 98 riders, representing 28 states and Canada, was cheered on by a large crowd, with estimates of numbers varying between 12,000 and 20,000 spectators.

The event, sanctioned by the American Motorcycle Association, was promoted as America's fastest road race. The day before the race was devoted to practice, and riders new to Daytona were in for a surprise. The backstretch was not straight, but featured three unexpected turns on the oiled beach road. Those who expected to coast were in for a big surprise, costing a few of them some paint and skin.

The following day, rested from an evening beachside oyster roast, 86 competitors lined up five abreast under perfect weather conditions.

Canadian E. Tony Miller, riding a Norton, took the early lead after receiving the green flag from veteran starter Jim Davis. Lester Hillbish, riding an Indian, was third, followed by another Indian rider, Ed Kretz, the winner of the 1936 race at Savannah. Kretz worked his way up from a starting position on the outside of the fifth row, took the lead at the end of the second lap in the turn exiting the beach and never looked back for his second consecutive victory in the 200—the first in Savannah, the second in Daytona Beach.

However, it wasn't an easy ride for Kretz, who thundered down the beach at more than 100 mph. At one point, a tail-wagging dog ran out onto the beach and into the path of the charging Californian, who guessed correctly which way to turn and missed the mongrel. Later in the race, the oncoming tide narrowed the south turn. Twice, Kretz was surprised by the higher water level while exiting the turn and spilled. Both times, he was quickly back on his mount, losing only about six seconds both times.

Kretz averaged an AMA record 71.10 mph, winning by five miles over Norton rider Clark Trumbull Jr. He needed two hours, 43 minutes and 37 seconds to complete the distance and collected $300 from the $750 purse.

Cummings, the reigning Indianapolis 500 winner who had participated in the 1936 stock-

car race, was among the finishers, recovering from a Friday practice spill to place 27th in his motorcycle debut.

The race was judged a success, both artistically and financially. "Daytona did itself proud in the matter of arrangements, a course, and climate," reported *The Motorcyclist*, the official publication of the AMA. "The Southeastern Dealers Association can be chalked up with the finest event in their series of class 'C' 200-mile road races."

Today, the Indianapolis 500, which dates back to 1911, is the only continuously running motorsports event that outranks the Daytona 200 by Arai.

There was another highlight that year, one that provided a link to the speed racers of earlier times. Joe Petrali established a motorcycle record of 136.183 mph on the measured mile on a specially built Harley-Davidson. The national champion's record has never been beaten at Daytona.

For France, the real news was that the track had stood up to the pounding of the motorcycles. Perhaps the marl could endure car tires. Prior to qualifying for the 1937 race, tons of it were hastily pounded into the turns in a routine resembling a modern pit stop. After all, the incoming tide would wash away the marl. Between the end of qualifying and the race, Volusia County road graders and steam rollers had to rush in, add the marl, pound it into the sand, then get back before racers sped through.

"It wasn't easy to do," France said. "We didn't know from one tide to the next what the beach was going to be like. We didn't know how much we were going to have to do to the straightaways. The tide would either raise or lower the beach, and this created a problem with our work on the turns. If you got a west wind, the tide would roughen the beach. If you got a sustained northeast wind, it would smooth the beach. It was never the same two days in a row."

To help ensure the tide would not wash away slower competitors or that the turns would become impassable despite the clay, the race was shortened to 50 miles.

To everyone's delight, the marl did its job. "The turns were dug up some at the point where the clay and the sand met," France said. "But, it was a definite improvement over the year before, and it gave us some idea where to go from there."

The temporary stands were filled even though there was no big purse to draw any famous names. Four South Carolina drivers joined 13 from Florida on September 5, 1937. Most again drove Fords, although there was a Plymouth, a Chevrolet, a Hudson and a Dodge mixed in.

C.D. "Smokey" Purser, owner of the local New York Bar & Grill, took home $43.56 for his victory.

Despite the meager purse, the Elks Club said it lost money and decided not to continue its sponsorship for 1938.

Daytona Beach, however, was not ready to give up on stock car races. "Without racing," said Ray Eberling, the city recreation officer, "Daytona Beach would be like a prize fighter with a wooden leg or a [baseball] pitcher with a wooden head."

At first, he found little more than a wooden nickel in his request for funds. Contacted by the city, prominent race promoter Ralph Hankinson, who promoted races in Pennsylvania and other northern tracks, estimated that putting on a good event would cost at least $20,000, a price tag that was hard to swallow during the Depression. Discussions with Hankinson ended quickly. In 1939, after France ran several successful races, Hankinson showed up to demand $10,000 from the city to officially "sanction" beach events. City Council chose France over Hankinson, both because France was a local resident and because he didn't ask for any public investment. Hankinson retaliated by banishing all southern drivers from his events, but had to give in when France went on a five-race victory tear in 1940, making him very popular and too good a draw to ban.

France wasn't included in the initial talks with Hankinson, but chatted with restaurant owner Charlie Reese about setting up a race in 1938. Reese was willing to invest

Motorcyclists had no trouble on the Beach Road Course turns. Bill France borrowed a technique for hardening the course, making it possible for stock car races to continue. Motorsports Images & Archives Photo

$1,000 if France served as promoter. Still inexperienced, France was reluctant to put on the whole show, so he decided to call Hankinson, who lived in a community about 20 miles southwest of Daytona Beach. A phone call there cost 25 cents, which was more than France wanted to spend. He tried making a collect call, but Hankinson declined to accept the charges.

"That's when I called Charlie Reese. It wasn't a toll call," France recalled, no doubt with a smile. "I decided to promote the race myself."

Hankinson's decision to reject the call eventually cost him billions of dollars.

France and Reese set an admission price of 50 cents and ended up with a $200 profit when some 5,000 people paid their way into the third beach race, which was moved from July 4 to July 10 because of rain.

The holiday date for the race was not a coincidence. Summers may be hot in Florida, but merchants rarely feel flush. Special events then and now were seen as a way to boost business. Spectators who came during what was normally a quiet season always needed rooms and food. Daytona Beach continues to host races during the July 4 holiday, even though the Florida sun can be brutal. The event was finally shifted to the evening in 1998, creating the best-attended, nighttime sporting event in the world.

The 1938 race went smoothly. The marl virtually eliminated the ruts, and 30 drivers participated, many with colorful nicknames like "Cannonball" Bob Baker, who worked at France's gas station; "Citrus" Charlie Herm; Woodrow "Pig" Ridings; and "Buttercup" Pearce. Once again, Fords dominated with only three Packards, two Auburns and a Hudson sprinkled through the lineup.

Mike Cone, who finished second in 1937, took advantage of the sunny weather when the race started and got a tan. He drove without a shirt.

A thunderstorm—another common hazard during Florida summer afternoons—intervened late in the race to add a little spice. With the tide due to arrive in an hour, France decided to ignore the rain and let the race continue. Cars slipped, slid and overturned in the wet conditions. Ed Eng wrapped his car around a telephone pole. Tommy Elmore, who probably won the 1936 race and insisted so for the rest of his life, tossed a wheel on the North Turn. Clyde Witt did that one better, losing two wheels from his Packard convertible. No one was hurt in any incidents.

Meanwhile, Danny Murphy, an Ormond Beach fireman, stayed in the lead by taking a slow, steady approach. France went into a sand dune; Purser, arguing that his fan belt had been sabotaged prior to the race, spent 20 minutes in the pits, then made up four laps on the leader. He still finished 15th.

Murphy won, taking home $300. France, who ended up second, had solicited area businesses to sponsor laps, so Murphy was awarded an additional $55 in prizes.

Everyone was happy except some city officials, who complained that some tourists were charged to go onto the beach while the race was on. "We cannot deny our visitors the privilege of using the beach at any time," officials intoned.

Since France and Reese actually turned a profit on the race, they decided to hold a second one, this time on the Labor Day weekend. The distance was increased to 156.8 miles. France added a $10 entry fee and required all drivers to participate in a 9 a.m. parade that weekend. The race actually was part of a series of holiday activities, including a boxing match, localized motorcycle races around barrels, junk car races around barrels and a rodeo.

This may have been the most important race France ever supervised. It vividly displayed his emerging style. He already knew that honesty was important. He recalled one race in which he finished third and received $10. Thinking back to a pre-race announcement in which the winner was promised $500, he asked the track officials if there were such a big disparity between first and third. He was told the $500 purse was only announced for public consumption. The winner actually received only $50.

"I remembered that," France said. Winners at his races would always receive the announced purse.

Then, there was the question of standards. France wanted to eliminate cheating and insisted every car be thoroughly inspected. He got a copy of the specs from the various companies "so we had something to match when we had the inspection after the race," he explained. "The manufacturers kept changing things, and we had a hard time keeping up with what was stock and what wasn't." As a result, inspections usually took longer than the race. The City Yard Garage was drafted for that purpose, and the examination of entries often took all night.

"They tore engines down and every part was checked," France said.

The examination was intensive. "One cylinder head would be removed, and the cylinder size would be examined. Pistons must not be .01 inches oversize. Compression ratio must be stock, and valve tension would also be checked," author Fielden noted. France's insistence on using only acceptable parts would definitely have an impact in 1938.

Despite the emphasis on the drivers, France did not overlook his audience. He knew who was really footing the bill. He purchased a 42-foot-high scoreboard so fans could stay abreast of race developments. "If the spectators are better informed, they will probably enjoy themselves more," France said. He erected grandstands outside the North Turn. An experimental sound system was added to keep everyone updated on what was happening on parts

of the course they couldn't see. Johnny Whitmore, otherwise unidentified, handled the public address system for the first race, the local newspaper noted.

To add interest, France also set up timing wires to record speeds. New records were always enticing gimmicks to draw a crowd. He was right on both counts. Speeds topped an entrancing 100 mph on the road section, while the attendance steadily climbed in succeeding years.

Again, France found a few lap sponsors, although cash wasn't the only prize. The leader on lap 28 got a box of cigars; beer went to the leader of lap 24.

Before a crowd estimated at 4,000, each of whom paid one dollar this time to get a seat, Purser jumped in front on lap 28 for good when leader Lloyd Moody was introduced to a sand dune. France came in second and Moody third.

As Reese waited to award the trophy to the winner, Purser simply drove by the reviewing stand and off the beach. In one version of what happened next, Ed Parkinson, head of the technical committee, became suspicious when Purser motored away. "We knew Smokey must have something on the car he didn't want checked," he said. "So, we got a few guys and went looking for him."

He said they found him in Roy Strange's garage, where the two men were hastily trying to remove some special high-compression heads popular in the Denver area. Purser recognized that they helped engines maintain power in the rarified Colorado air. At ground level, the nonstandard equipment gave Purser's car a real boost.

In a second tale, supported by newspaper accounts, no one tailed Purser to the garage. Instead, Purser showed up at the track three hours later, about 3:50 p.m., insisting he was not supposed to have his car inspected until 4 p.m. By then, however, according to Fielden, the drivers had already voted unanimously to disqualify him. The *Daytona*

Motorcycle racers ran their first beach event in 1936. The Daytona 200 By Arai remains the foremost motorcycle race in the country. Motorsports Images & Archives Photo

TIRES

NASCAR's founder Bill France probably said it best: "You can't race without tires." Whether tires fell off or were glued on, they are an absolute necessity—from the first race in 1903 through modern times. No one can set a speed record or visit victory lane without them. Daytona would not exist as the capital of motorsports without them.

The first tires were an outgrowth of the rubber industry that had existed for more than a century before the original automobile tested the road. Columbus even brought some rubber back with him as proof of his cross-Atlantic journey. In the 1700s, chemist Joseph Priestly, who discovered oxygen, figured out that the sap drawn from certain tropical trees "rubbed" out pencil marks better than the stale bread crumbs then being used. The name "rubber" stuck.

Because of the product's versatility, many manufacturers tried to come up with uses. Products made from this sticky material, however, would often melt in warm weather and crack in cold weather. While melting, it also gave off a terrible odor. Yet rubber was so flexible that scientists experimented with ways to get it to hold its shape regardless of the temperature.

Charles Goodyear managed the feat in 1839 by accidentally dropping a rubber-sulfur mixture onto a stove. At least, that's the story put out by Goodyear Tire & Rubber Co., which was founded in 1898 and named for the inventor. The heat solidified the rubber. Goodyear, a Connecticut native, tested the durability of his "vulcanized" rubber by placing the compound on his back porch. It was still resilient the next day despite the New England chill. By chance—supposedly the impov-erished scientist using the stove to hide his rubber experiment from his wife—Goodyear had created a product that was stable, tough and resilient.

His success did him little good. Goodyear died deeply in debt.

Fortunately, his work was not ignored. In the mid-1840s, Englishman Robert William Thomson patented the pneumatic tire, essentially a hollow belt inflated with air. The patent describes it as "the application of elastic bearings around the wheels of carriages, rendering their motion easier and diminishing the noise they made while in motion." He created the tire—short for "attire" of a wheel—by using several layers of canvas, saturated with rubber and vulcanized.

In the 1880s, an Irish veterinarian independently created a tire for his son's tricycle. John Boyd Dunlop's inflatable rubber tubes were held onto rims with wrapped tape. Soon after, Charles Welch devised a method of fastening a tire to the rim by using a continuous, rubber-coat strand of wire (bead) in the thickening edge of the casing.

Dunlop kept buying up patents and introduced its tires into the United States by the mid-1890s under license of the Diamond Rubber Co. Hartford Rubber Co. made tires in this country based on its own bicycle tires and following the Dunlop design. Hartford's were the brand J. Frank Duryea used in 1895 to win the inaugural American automobile race.

The first truly American tire was the G & J, patented by Thomas N. Jeffrey in 1892 and sold by Gormully and Jeffrey, which originally manufactured the Ramble bicycle.

In 1896, B.F. Goodrich produced the first

pneumatic tires designed specifically for cars. It was called the Winton, named for famed racer Alexander Winton. A surgeon, Goodrich took over the Hudson River Tire Co. and moved it to Akron, a small city in northeast Ohio. Located along the Cuyahoga River, it was close to the Erie Canal, train lines and a central spot between major cities like New York, Chicago and Cleveland. The Seiberling brothers founded Goodyear Tire & Rubber Co., which now outfits all NASCAR cars and trucks, and followed Goodrich to Ohio. The Seiberlings eventually left Goodyear to start a company under their own name. Henry Firestone, whose namesake company is now owned by Japan's Bridgestone Tire Co., started his own business in Akron in 1903. Several major tire companies still have their headquarters in "the Rubber Capital of the World" even though no tires are manufactured there now.

A newcomer to racing, Hoosier Tires didn't start producing tires until 1957. Bob Newton and his wife, Joyce, began by retreading street tires with softer compounds, working from an old, abandoned horse barn in South Bend, Indiana. The name "Hoosier" was chosen to reflect the origin of Newton's racing roots on Midwest short tracks. The purple color associated with the company came from the color of his No. 4 race car.

In 1978, the company opened the world's first and only factory singularly devoted to the production of racing tires.

Initially, tire companies strengthened their rubber products with fabric, such as Irish linen or Egyptian cotton. However, the cross fibers of woven materials generate heat as they chafe against each other while under pressure. Eventually, the heat undermined the stability of the tire. The solution was an all-warp fabric invented in 1893. "The threads, or cords, were laid parallel on the sheet rubber without touching each other," according to an unattributed history of tires. Giovanni Batista Pirelli patented his fabric tires in 1894.

To overcome side stresses, the cords were turned at an angle to the rim. The resulting bias tire was given the name Silvertown after the site of the London tire-making factory. That same name is still used by B.F. Goodrich, which bought the American rights to the tire.

Today, most tires follow a radial design in which the cords run from bead to bead in a straight line. Radial tires tend to run straighter with better mileage and less wear.

Various ideas, including metal and leather, were devised to create treads to protect the tire from the innumerable and annoying punctures. In the late 1800s, Michelin came up with the most imitated approach, a 1/6-inch layer of leather that was tapered at the edges and cemented to the rubber and fabric. Walnut shells were once added to the tread to add grip in racing tires for such strenuous events like climbs of Pike's Peak. Metal was used in cold climates.

At one time, leather was considered as a replacement for rubber. It offered a long life, but had the propensity to crack in the cold. Paper was tested, too, along with wood. Manufacturers also experimented with various substitutes for air, including a heavy fluid that gelled such as soybean oil or a porous, elastic compound. Sponge rubber was considered; so was cork, sawdust, shellac, asbestos and arsenic.

After more than 100 years, however, no one has come up with a better product to carry a speeding automobile than a circle composed of rubber and filled with air.

Beach Morning Journal reported the disqualification was caused "because he failed to bring his car to the garage immediately after the race."

Purser said he "had to stop at his place of business" before having the car inspected.

The end result was the same, regardless of the actual sequence: Purser was disqualified. France, who came in second, was declared the winner. However, Reese didn't think the promoter should get the first-place check, so the money went to Moody, who finished third.

Purser was livid. "They checked my car before the race and passed it okay," he pointed out. "They knew what my car was before the race started. If they felt it was not stock then, they should not have let me run."

He dismissed a problem found in his car during inspection. Officials said the compression ratio in one cylinder was 132 pounds before the race and 99 pounds afterwards. Specifications allowed 129 pounds. "The cylinders checked different due to the fact of a hard grind of the race," insisted Purser, who also attributed the change to a "special oil" used in the engine.

The disqualification stuck. Working against Purser was his reputation for cutting corners wherever he could. Enormously popular, he boasted about being a bootlegger during Prohibition and bringing in illegal alcohol via boats to Daytona Beach.

The brouhaha did not die down immediately. Purser continued to call himself the 1938 winner. Race promotions for the 1939 races also advertised that Purser was the defending champion. In addition to demanding adherence to rigid regulations, France was learning about promotions—the resulting publicity helped boost interest in future events.

More importantly, he and Reese split $2,000 profit after the second 1938 race. "That was more money than I had ever seen at one time before," France said.

He would never undervalue racing again.

A fierce competitor, Bill France (right) charges through the deepening grooves in 1936 during the first race on the Beach-Road Course.Motorsports Images & Archives Photo

chapter seven

1939-40

France marched into 1939 with more plans. For starters, drivers were allowed to fiddle with the compression ratio, exactly what Purser had done the year before. Purser immediately took advantage of the change by claiming to install an Indianapolis 500 engine in his Ford.

For the first 1939 race, held March 19 and extending 156.8 miles, "Cannonball" Baker won the pole, but he had some experience at speeding. Local police had given him a $10 ticket for reckless driving on a city street earlier in the month.

France grabbed the lead and held it through a mid-race pit stop. Most cars never needed to stop. France was the only driver who pitted in the entire race. His pause was for only 11 seconds, which would have been fine, but someone in his makeshift crew failed to add enough fuel. After a forced second stop, he ended up far behind winner Sam Rice. Purser, by the way, had a normal engine in his car.

In the second race, a 160-miler held July 4, Stuart Joyce flipped going into the South Turn on lap 28. He righted himself with the help of spectators and caught France and Purser for the win. He took home $350 and averaged a record 76.03 mph.

On a roll, France and Reese put on a third race on Labor Day weekend. This time, the race was only 102.4 miles, and cars radically altered for racing ("cut down") were banned.

Jimmy Gibson was supposed to start on the pole but got caught in holiday traffic. With 10,000 people trying to get to the race, cars were backed up for miles from the highway to the beach. The green flag waved at 2 p.m. without him.

France started off in front, but ended up having to get water to cool an overheating engine with only six laps left. Purser passed him. France finished only a handful of yards behind at the finish line.

OPPOSITE: **Ralph Earnhardt shows off the rudimentary cockpit of an early race car. Cars were often taken directly from a car lot, given a safety belt and put on the track.**
Motorsports Images and Archives Photo

"Smokey's car was nothing special," reported the *Daytona Beach Evening Journal*. "It's the family car with the hub caps and bumpers off. After the race, he loaded up the family and took them home."

In 1940, as the war already underway in Europe loomed on the horizon, 10,000 people turned out on March 10 to watch the first race that year. "Rapid" Roy Hall, 19, came down from Atlanta with Bob Flock to challenge the local drivers and rode away with the win.

According to the Living Legends of Auto Racing Inc., which was founded by "Cannonball" Baker's daughter-in-law, Atlanta police chased Hall for two years for running illegal liquor, speeding, and reckless driving. "He was a genius at the wheel," one officer said.

Hall's car was prepared by Louis Jerome "Red" Vogt, who years later came up with the NASCAR name.

Hall boasted that he drove from Atlanta to Daytona Beach in seven hours and averaged 62 mph—an impressive feat before the days of interstate highways. A few days later, he thrilled race fans by running his car on two wheels through the North and South Turns. Mayor Ucal Cunningham may not have been as enchanted. Hall's unrestrained driving threw sand across the distinguished guests in the front box seats, including His Honor.

The key to victory again was found in the pits. Race leader Joe Littlejohn had a standard two-minute pit stop on lap 29. Hall pitted on the 36th lap, and Vogt got him out in 40 seconds. As a result, Hall won by half a lap and set a new race record of 76.53 mph.

Hall, whose career was cut short by injuries in 1949, remained a local legend. In 1946, he showed up three days before the June race and was immediately arrested for speeding and cutting donuts on Main Street. "He explained that he wanted to go to the local jail because the Daytona hotel rates were too high," according to a Living Legends report.

While Hall led most of the race, many novice drivers discovered that the dunes were nearby and that the sand could be slippery. They tumbled over the small, sandy hills, got themselves righted and back in the race. Larry Grant flipped his Willys in a spectacular crash, was knocked unconscious and put in an ambulance. He promptly clamored out, got bystanders to help him upright his car and finished 15th.

Once again, the 32 entrants for the 160-mile race mostly drove Fords.

In the second race, held on July 7, France led all 160 miles from start to finish in his final victory on the beach. He drove a Buick, one of several in the race, insisting he held back on the throttle because he was "afraid the spectators would not like the idea" of the promoter winning the race.

The 39-car field was becoming more diversified. Lloyd Moody, who ended far back in the field, drove a GMC pickup truck.

Mishaps, as usual, were common. C.P. McDonald drove into the ocean after his car caught on fire. George Ruse Jr. fell off the pace in his Chevrolet pickup truck when an elderly woman—another source said two people were involved—wandered onto the course. Ruse Jr. swerved to avoid her and got stuck in the sand. "The old woman didn't even help me get un-stuck," he complained.

With crowds burgeoning, France put on a third race in 1940, and then added an all-women's 25.6-miler on September 1. His wife, Anne, was one of the competitors. France stationed flagmen along the curves in hopes of slowing down the drivers and reducing possible injuries. The women ignored the flagmen completely. Grace McLendon, described as "a former Daytona Beach bathing beauty," overshot the beach and almost ran over one of the frustrated flagmen. She had won the

In 1954, Curtis Turner (No. 14) skitters through the old North Turn with a trio of cars on his rear bumper, including Herb Thomas (92 Jr), who eventually finished second. Tommy Elliott (No. 97A) had plenty of time to enjoy the action as his car ended up on one of the dunes. Fans on the south side of the track paid to get in; those who gathered on the beach probably didn't. **Motorsports Images & Archives Photo**

1937 Miss Daytona Beach title.

The winner, Evelyn Reed, averaged 68.4 mph for the victory. The *Daytona Beach Morning Journal* labeled her a "heavy-footed miss." She won $50, a permanent wave and several prizes. "These gals could handle the race cars," author Fielden noted. "A few of the male observers must have felt ashamed."

For the men's event the next day, France changed the rules again. To prevent a big car, like his Buick, from dominating, he and co-promoter Smokey Purser decreed that all entries must cost less than $1,100 with engines that produced less

than 120 hp.

He needed an exciting race, having decided to schedule his event on the same day as an important race in Atlanta. After several key Georgia drivers chose to come to Florida, including Bob Flock, France knew he had a winner.

Rain forced a delay in the start, and the race was reduced to 105.6 miles.

Buster Mathis, a local gas station owner in only his second race, won. Littlejohn, who ended up behind Purser in third, protested that the two cars in front of him were illegal. France had all three cars inspected and found that none of them were

Driver Johnny Stolpmann (No. 93) checks his equipment prior to the start of a Beach Road Course race. Races were held on the beach from 1936 through 1958. Many of the early competitors are only known today by the name painted on the side of their cars. Motorsports Images & Archives Photo

"strictly stock." However, to avoid another situation like had occurred in 1938, he declared the finishing order was correct.

"I had no idea my car didn't meet specifications," Littlejohn said. "Actually, I withdrew my protest. I offered to let 'em keep the third-place money, if they gave my $25 protest fee and three-dollar entry fee back."

Despite his casual approach, the jovial aura surrounding the races slowly was becoming shadowed by a dark cloud rolling in from across the same ocean that lapped at the edges of the beach course. As 1941 began, the United States was increasingly being drawn into World War II. The Japanese attack on Pearl Harbor was only a few months away, while this government was already busily helping England, then standing virtually alone against the Nazi onslaught.

France tied his March 2, 1941 race into the growing conflict by setting up a "Bundles for Britain" charity event. More than 10,000 people attended. Reflecting how significant the races on the beach had become, about half of the 44 cars in the field were piloted by former champions, including France, who was the 1940 national driving champion.

The cars started four abreast. Bill Snowden was forced to go to a borrowed car after hitting a passenger car during his qualifying run. The motorist who wandered onto the course "must have been terribly lost," racing historian Fielden commented.

He wasn't the only spectator trying to avoid the race cars. With crowds jammed alongside the course, there was little room to move when trouble occurred.

On lap 14, Littlejohn skidded across the lip of the North Turn and into the crowd. For the first time since races resumed in 1936, the yellow caution flag waved. At least five spectators were hurt, two hospitalized.

Soon after, Jap Brogdon and Massey Atkins collided and flipped their open-roof cars. Massey's car struck the wooden box seats. Elbert Etkins roared into the South Turn and barely made it through, brushing against a soon-to-be-embarrassed fan watching along the rim. The car's fender "caught the spectator's pants leg and tore it off" the morning Daytona Beach newspaper reported the next day.

The cars seemed to aim at the stands. Race announcer Sam Nunis said he spent most of the event on the move. "I dropped the mike and ran like hell for the bushes every time a car came around," he recalled. "One car hit our stand, and it shook like a tree in a typhoon."

Hall again beat back such stalwarts as Fontello (Fonty) Flock and Jap Brogden. Prize money only went so far: the 16th-place finisher, Marvel Gallentine from New Smyrna Beach, "won three pairs of socks," according to the *Daytona Beach Morning Journal*.

France didn't sit around when the checkered flag waved. He added a wooden crash fence to shield spectators and scheduled a second race for the end of the month. He called it the Frank Lockhart Memorial to honor the speed racer killed back in 1928.

Another huge crowd, estimated at 12,000, showed up to watch France lead 45 cars into the first turn. The fence was quickly tested as "Crazy" Cy Clark, described later as a "hell-bent-for-leather lunatic," swept over the rim of the turn into the fence. Moments later, much-abused Mayor Cunningham had broken pieces of the fence and a 1939 Mercury virtually in his lap.

Purser finally held off Hall in a side-by-side duel for his third official win. "That ol' man drove a helluva race," Hall said.

A third race was set up for July 27. Another

innovation was added. The field was limited to 33 cars, paralleling the Indianapolis 500. France also allowed Purser in the race, although the popular driver failed to qualify.

Lloyd Seay, Hall's cousin, flipped his car, landed on all four tires and kept going. Ruse Jr. sailed over the bank of the North Turn and stopped against a support post beneath the grandstand there. Fonty Flock was injured in a crash that kept him from racing for six years.

Substitute Bernie Long took advantage of a cut tire that slowed then-leader Bill Snowden to grab the victory.

With time still left in 1941, a fourth race was added to the schedule. Seay jumped from 15th to first on the first lap and led all 160 miles. The Georgian, only 21, was on a three-race winning streak when, later that year, he was shot to death in a fight over sugar content in the family-owned moonshine business.

The end of the race was soon followed by the start of World War II for Americans. The local newspaper reported, "War delivered a knockout blow to Daytona Beach's spectacular sports events...Due to restrictions upon the use of tires and the fact that we all want to conserve and cooperate with the government to the limit, the races on the Beach-Road course have been cancelled."

France, who was deep in planning the 1942

Promoters set up races wherever they could find a suitable site, including small dirt tracks where clouds of dust blocked vision. Motorsports Images & Archives Photo

Fonty Flock (No. 1) ended up high and dry in an early race on the Beach Road Course. Motorsports Images & Archives Photo

events when the war started, issued a statement with his partner, Reese: "The stock car races call for the use of fuel, rubber and many motor parts, and mechanical workers all needed to win the war."

The war curtailed the motorcycle races, too. They had continued side by side with the stock car events.

Ben Campanale of Pomona, California, won both in 1938 and 1939. He needed 2:42:10 to complete the 200 miles on his Harley-Davidson, winning by one minute over Les Hillbish of Reading, Pennsylvania, who was just ahead of Tom Hayes of Dallas, Texas. The crowd was up from the inaugural event, the course smoother, and the number of entries increased to 125.

Campanale lowered his time to 2:36:28 in 1939, winning over Ray Eddy of San Francisco on a Harley-Davidson and Bill Anderson of Houston on an Indian. Sam Arena traded the lead with Campanale several times, before a spill got sand in his engine and took him out of the race.

The course was overhauled for 1940, with a new type of dirt mixture applied to the turns, overlaid with calcium chloride to keep down the dust. Rhode Island Harley-Davidson rider Babe Tancrede won in 2:39:45, followed by Daytona's Wally Akins on an Indian, and Paul Brown of Jacksonville on a Harley.

Billy Matthews of Hamilton, Ontario won the 1941 race on a Norton in the fastest time to date, 2:33:41. Tancrede finished second in an unsuccessful bid for a third straight Daytona 200 victory.

After that race, the beach was quiet, still waiting, as young competitors picked up weapons and sailed into battle, and the older men picked up tools and went back to work.

F.F. Frederick (No. 47) skitters through the turn in the Beach Road Course, obscuring the vision of the driver in the car (No. 17) to his left. Motorsports Images & Archives Photo

WOMEN BEHIND THE WHEEL

While 13 women competed in the 1941 race, the event was considered an exhibition. Women wanted more than that. When several women sent in entry forms for the July race at Daytona Beach in 1949, several men objected.

Bill France listened to the complaints, then ruled women could participate on an equal basis. "France had decided that the woman auto racer is here to stay, like the atom bomb, rum and home hair waves," The *Daytona Beach News Journal* reported.

Ethel Flock Mobley, sister of Tim, Bob and Fonty Flock, competed in that 1949 race. Named after the gasoline her father used in his taxi, according to the Living Legends of Auto Racing Inc., Mobley was the youngest daughter in the Flock family. For the most part, she limited her racing to the Atlanta area, except for the 1949 Firecracker 400 in Daytona Beach. She drove a 1949 Cadillac to an 11th-place finish in a field of 26—ahead of Herb Thomas, Curtis Turner and her brothers, Bob and Fonty.

"She particularly loved racing with and beating her brothers," Tim Flock said.

Her success brought other women into racing, including Sara Christian of Atlanta, who started her career in 1949. She drove a 1949 Oldsmobile, prepared by her husband, Frank. Her best finish was fifth in the October race at Heidelberg, Pennsylvania. It remains the only top-five NASCAR finish for a woman. Christian also had two top-10 finishes and was named Woman Driver of the Year in 1949.

Another top female racer was Louise Smith from Georgia, who won a variety of modified races and was the first woman elected to the Motorsports Hall of Fame in Talladega, Alabama.

Janet Guthrie, who in 1976 became the first woman in 21 years to race in the NASCAR Winston Cup Series, is perhaps the best known of all the women racers. The veteran sports car driver turned to NASCAR when she failed to qualify for the 1976 Indianapolis 500. She landed a ride in a Hoss Ellington Chevrolet for the Coca-Cola 600 at Lowe's Motor Speedway and qualified 27th, just behind Dale Earnhardt and Bill Elliott. Guthrie finished 15th, prompting Charlotte businesswoman Linda Ferreri to purchase the car and field it for the 1977 campaign.

Driving a green Kelly Services Chevrolet fielded by Ferreri, Guthrie opened 1977 with a 12th-place finish in the Daytona 500, and was the top rookie. She recorded 10 top-12 finishes in 10 starts, with her best finish a sixth at Bristol Motor Speedway. After attempting to compete in both Indy Car and NASCAR races, Guthrie resigned her USAC license to concentrate on NASCAR Winston Cup competition. A leader in the Raybestos Rookie of the Year competition early in the season, she finished third behind Ricky Rudd and Sam Sommers, and 23rd in the NASCAR Winston Cup standings.

"I really, really loved NASCAR racing and I had a wonderful time," Guthrie recalled. "It took about a year, but the guys came around and started treating me like just another driver. I remember in May 1977, it finally happened, when everyone finally stopped looking at me squinty-eyed every time I walked through the garage."

Along the way, Guthrie scored other personal highlights, including outqualifying "King" Richard Petty at Talladega Superspeedway and leading the season finale at Ontario Motor Speedway. She holds the NASCAR record for starts (33) by a woman and top-10 finishes (five).

Ironically, despite finishing 1977 on a high note, Guthrie failed to garner sponsorship for an encore. After limited NASCAR Winston Cup competition in 1978 and 1979 (years in which she also raced in the Indianapolis 500), she drove a Texaco-sponsored car owned by Rodney Osterland in the 1980 Daytona 500 and recorded an 11th-place finish. Her teammate, NASCAR Winston Cup championship-bound Dale Earnhardt, placed fourth. Without sponsorship, her only other NASCAR Winston Cup drive came later that year, when she drove an uncompetitive car at Pocono Raceway.

Robin McCall was the next female to compete in NASCAR Winston Cup competition, driving in both Michigan races in 1982. Road racer Patty Moise drove in five NASCAR Winston Cup races, beginning with the 1987 event at Watkins Glen International to the 1989 Talladega 500 at Talladega Superspeedway.

In 2001, Shawna Robinson became the 15th woman to enter the NASCAR Winston Cup Series when she tried to qualify the Aaron's Rent Ford for the NAPA AUTO PARTS 400 at California Speedway in April 2001. Her car broke down, but the Iowa native went on to drive in a race at Michigan International Speedway.

The highest finish to date by any female competitor in major oval track competition occurred in 2001 when Sarah Fisher, who competes in the Indy Racing League, recorded a second-place finish at Homestead-Miami Speedway.

More than one woman has competed in a single NASCAR NEXTEL Cup race. In 1950, Louise Smith, Ann Chester and Christian competed in an event in Hamburg (N.Y.) Fairgrounds. In 1977, Lella Lombardi, Christine Becker and Guthrie all drove in the annual Pepsi 400 at Daytona International Speedway.

"There's no physical reason why the NASCAR Winston Cup champion can't be a woman," said Mark Martin, a veteran competitor who joined NASCAR's elite series in 1981, left and then returned in 1988.

The problem comes with experience, he said. Little girls aren't encouraged to go into motorsports.

"It is difficult to break into," Martin continued. "It is difficult to work your way through the short track and all the way up through NASCAR to be a champion."

Here are the women to date who made the climb into NASCAR's elite series.

Name	Years	No. of Races
Christine Beckers	1977	1
Ann Bunselmeyer	1950	1
Ann Chester	1950	2
Sara Christian	1949-1950	7
Janet Guthrie	1976-1980	33
Lella Lombardi	1977	1
Robin McCall	1982	2
Ethel Mobley	1949	2
Patty Moise	1987-1989	5
Marian Pagan	1954	1
Goldie Parsons	1965	1
Shawna Robinson	2001-2002	8
Ann Slaasted	1950	1
Fifi Scott	1955	2
Louise Smith	1949-1950	11

Sand obscured everything as defending NASCAR champ Bill Rexford (No. 61) leads the field through the North Turn on the 1951 Beach Road Course race. Bill Snowden (No. 16) is right behind. Local favorite and future Hall of Fame driver Marshall Teague started sixth, but came on to win the 160-mile event by more than a minute. Motorsports Images & Archives Photo

chapter eight

AFTER THE WAR

Bill France spent the war working on submarine chasers in a South Beach Street boatyard. Other motorsports figures got closer to the action.

Robert "Red" Byron, a Colorado native who grew up in Alabama, was a sergeant in the army air corps and suffered a badly injured leg after being shot down on his 58th mission. Doctors didn't know if he'd ever walk again. Marshall Teague, a Daytona Beach native, joined the army air corps and ended up as a lieutenant while making bombing runs in the Far East. Russ Truelove served in the U.S. Navy; Curtis "Crawfish" Crider was in the U.S. Air Force.

When the fighting ended in 1945, stock car racing resumed outside Daytona Beach almost immediately in a burst of postwar enthusiasm. The roar of engines replaced the screech of Stukas and the blast of mortars. The promoters tended to be a tawdry group. Historian Tuthill called them "mostly a bunch of numbers guys and bootleggers. There weren't big purses." Most of the money that circulated in the races was wagered in the stands.

The days when the wealthy sportsmen started up their engines to compete in gentlemanly races were forgotten in the mist of time. Gone, too, was the properly coiffed speed racer with a scarf artistically draped around his neck. The competitors "were pretty desperate characters, most of them," Tuthill said. "They were outrunning cops and being shot at…" Legendary mechanic Red Vogt built cars for moonshiners on one side of his Atlanta garage and cars for revenuers on the other side, according to driver Crider.

Some tracks banned drivers with police records. At one Georgia track, Bob Flock, who had been charged with hauling moonshine, slipped onto the track in the back straightaway and set off a Keystone Kop chase with police tearing after him. Flock finally went through the pits and was caught after running out of gas in midtown Atlanta.

On April 14, 1946, France returned to motorsports and presented another beach race. This time he was working alone. Reese had died in 1945. The event drew 10,000 fans and

Carl Burris (No. 19) strains to catch up with Wayne
Jackson (No. 3) in a 1951 Modified race. Both finished in
the top 50 in a race that drew more than 100 entries.
Motorsports Images & Archives Photo

many of the top drivers participated, including Byron, Teague and Buddy Shuman, another driver with a checkered past. After failing to outrun a deputy sheriff in North Carolina, Shuman had been shot in the throat and spent some time on a chain gang.

The war years had not been good to the old Beach Road Course. France wanted to hold the race in March, but needed another month to get ready because of all the damage. The stands in the North and South Turns had vanished. To replace them, France rented bleachers from the Ringling Brothers circus that wintered in Sarasota. Seating was limited, and France encouraged spectators to park their cars on the beach.

Many of the drivers were familiar to local fans. Littlejohn, on the pole after clocking 94.1 mph, had been in starting grids since 1938. Roy Hall was out of jail and back from Atlanta. Byron showed up despite his mangled left leg. To compensate for the injury, his left boot was bolted to a specially designed clutch.

About 7,500 people paying $1.50 each were on hand to welcome back the racers after 1,697

days of quiet. Littlejohn led the field into the North Turn, but Hall and Byron soon took charge. Byron lost time by hitting a fence on lap 17, while Hall had to pull himself from the surf. The two dueled until Hall threw a tire in the South Turn and crashed at the halfway mark. Byron led the last 25 laps for the victory with France coming home fifth.

A second race was held in June. Hall won $1,000 and the 102.4-mile event by driving straight through without a pit stop. Bill France pulled off his helmet for the last time, admitting he could drive or promote, but not both.

He wasn't the only veteran to call it quits.

Purser, Cy Clark and Stewart Joyce, Mike Cone, Tommy Elmore all announced their retirements, although Purser came back after a few years to compete in several races before breaking his right arm in a final run.

This was a young person's sport. France said "Driving 160 miles on the Beach Road Course is about as easy as driving nonstop across the continent."

The old-timers were soon replaced by drivers eager to carve their own names into racing history—Gober Sosebee, Lee Petty, Curtis Turner and Buck Baker.

There was no Labor Day race that year. Amid a surging economy and returning GIs, racing seemed more of a nuisance in a city where the sport was born. Complaints about the noise from local merchants and residents forced the cancellation. France took the drivers to other tracks, but was back in Daytona Beach in January 1947.

In that race, Byron slid into the lead, held off an array of competitors and finished with a substantial lead. The event was the first to be filmed for newsreels. A second race, held in March, saw a falloff

Before development filled the beach with high-rise condominiums, the annual race on the beach drew large crowds to the southern part of the peninsula. To reduce walk-ons, Bill France posted signs warning spectators to "Beware of Rattlesnakes." Motorsports Images & Archives Photo

in interest, possibly because of bad weather, but more likely because ticket prices were boosted to $4.50. France quickly lowered the admission price for the next races.

In June, Roy Hall returned to claim a victory. A local racer, however, made the biggest impression. Glenn "Fireball" Roberts, who would become NASCAR's first icon, finished in the top 10 and attracted attention by showing little regard for life, limb or car. Then, he was an employee in Marshall Teague's garage and would later work in a carburetor factory. His nickname came from his high school baseball-pitching prowess but seemed to foreshadow his death in a fiery crash less than 16 years later.

The caterwauling from nearby residents, however, forced France to reconsider the Beach Road Course. It had served him well since 1936, but developers were closing in. "It was getting so built up near the course that we decided to move down the peninsula as far as we could go," he recalled.

He already knew that beach racing was ready to see its last checkered flag and would inform city leaders of that fact in 1953. In 1954, he would announce the last year of racing, only to repeat that claim through 1958. Still, the end was in sight. New homes and commercial buildings were springing up. The value of beach property had jumped. "I figured that the farther south we went, the longer we could race on the beach," France said.

His new course, opened in 1948, essentially started at Wilbur by the Sea, an unincorporated community south of Daytona Beach Shores. It resembled the previous one, but was longer and featured an extra exit, creating a track inside a track. Motorcycles were scheduled to use the full course, which stretched 4.1 miles. Cars initially turned off at the first exit, racing 2.2 miles a lap.

New bleachers were added, but were subject to the usual abuse from the weather. "They were permanent in only the vaguest sense of the word," France said. "Like the others, a good, strong wind would come up and blow them down."

With the welter of champions, varied track conditions and dubious promotions, racing itself also needed a more solid edifice. France was determined to build one. In many ways, he had started to without realizing it. His skill at attracting customers had generated calls from various tracks struggling to draw crowds. They looked enviously at the

In 1949, Red Byron competed in six races, winning two and claiming the first NASCAR championship. He won the title in both the stock car and modified divisions. Motorsports Images & Archives Photo

In the early years of NASCAR, cars that competed in races, including these lined up on the sand in Daytona Beach, Florida, in 1950, were often driven off the lot directly into competition. **Motorsports Images & Archives Photo**

thousands turning out to see a race on the beach and figured France could help them achieve the same success.

France would comply, ending up with a fledgling series. "I organized eight or 10 races in 1947 under the name National Champion Stock Car Circuit," France said. The series' motto was: "Where the fastest that run, run the fastest."

The series was supervised from his home by his wife, Anne, who had become an active partner in organizing and directing the races. France was not sure if interest was strong enough to form a more permanent organization, but he decided to find out.

He contacted motorsports leaders in various communities and invited them to a meeting in Daytona Beach in 1947. After the war, France had bought the lounge on the top of the Streamline Hotel, then the tallest structure on the beach. The facility is still there. Racers used to gather in France's bar to swap stories about past exploits and exchange information about upcoming events. The meeting, which would change the history of racing, took place in the Ebony Room located above the lounge.

France, listed as director, gaveled the First Annual Convention of the National Championship Stock Car Circuit to order at 1 p.m., Sunday, December 14. The minutes from the meeting are still extant. They show that 18 representatives from Atlanta, Boston, Providence, New York, and Washington, D.C. made the trip along with track operators from smaller towns in Ohio, New Jersey, Florida and South Carolina. Eight more men would arrive Monday and Tuesday to join those already on hand. Eventually, according to historian Fielden, 35 men participated.

One of them was a driver named Sam Packard, the last survivor of the group. The New Englander, then 28, later recorded his recollections in a 1998 issue of NASCAR *Winston Cup Scene Illustrated*. He said participants didn't bring paper, so everyone scribbled notes on cocktail napkins.

Bill Tuthill, a former race-car driver and promoter, was named temporary chairman and, Packard said, did a lot of the talking. Tuthill had moved to Ormond Beach in the 1940s and was the first writer to chronicle the beach races.

France outlined his goals for the group. "There are a whole lot of things to straighten out here," He told them. "We've got to get track owners and promoters interested in building up stock car racing. Stock car racing as we've been running it is not, in my opinion, the answer. I believe stock car racing can become a nationally recognized sport by having a national point standing, which embraces the majority of large stock car events."

He had no doubt about the significance of the meeting. "Right here, within our group, rests the outcome of stock car racing in the country today. We have the opportunity to set it up on a big scale," France said.

Packard, who had worked for France at his gas station, didn't recognize that big a picture. "No one had any idea we were creating history those four days in December," he said. "No one ever thought it could get so big."

The *2001 NASCAR Media Guide* agreed: "Not even France, who believed a sanctioning body was exactly what the sport of stock car racing needed, could have envisioned what NASCAR has become today."

That's understandable. The new organization started with enthusiasm and little else. Marshall Teague was authorized to countersign any checks, a necessary precaution weakened by the basic fact the new organization had no money. Tuthill and promoter Ed Otto bought shares in NASCAR,

helping provide some money for the coffers, and were later bought out by France.

Lacking resources, the group set up committees. They also voted to call themselves the National Stock Car Racing Association (NSCRA). Vogt recommended another name, the National Association of Stock Car Auto Racing (NASCAR), but heard complaints that his suggestion sounded too much like "Nash-Car." However, someone later recalled that there was already a group in Georgia that used the NSCRA moniker. NASCAR won on a re-vote.

Vogt wasn't being totally original. He had helped start another group in Georgia, called the Georgia Association of Stock Car Auto Racing (GASCAR). He recommended that France simply substitute the word "National" for "Georgia," according to Frank Thomas, an early car inspector and race starter who worked with GASCAR. GASCAR faded quickly from the scene as NASCAR began to grow.

Many of the nation's top race promoters met in 1947 to found NASCAR. Bill France (center) led the organization and served as president. Motorsports Images & Archives Photo

Three NASCAR leaders got together for the camera in 1948, the year the sanctioning body promoted its first races: (from left) Red Vogt, a master mechanic who suggested the NASCAR name; NASCAR founder Bill France; and the first NASCAR champion Red Byron. **Motorsports Images & Archives Photo**

The new organization's slogan became "Racing that is open to everyone."

It may have been, but not everyone wanted in. Representatives from existing groups, several of whom came to the inaugural gathering, had no intention of joining.

To counter them and to make sure any new rules were followed, France needed power. He got it by having NASCAR incorporated as a private company with him as president. The streamlined operation meant France could handle tasks without going through a possibly contentious committee, something that had hamstrung previous attempts to organize. He appointed a race steward at each event. The same individual was assigned to handle insurance claims. No fuss, no discussion.

"We had our own man at the track," Tuthill said. "Since he wasn't elected but appointed, it was simple.

"If he didn't do the job, we dis-appointed him."

Insurance may have been the fledgling group's strongest asset. No other racing organization offered insurance. Moreover, NASCAR paid the claim, then submitted its own paperwork to insurance companies. That was an astonishing advance and tremendously popular with the drivers, who usually showed up at races with little more than the few dollars in their pockets. "In most cases," France pointed out, "drivers ended up as charity cases unless they could pay their bills."

The novel insurance approach created instant credibility. "Suddenly," Tuthill explained, "here was a racing organization that paid hospital bills. Doctors were being paid, and it gave NASCAR a tremendous amount of stature."

In addition, NASCAR's officers made sure that all the income was accounted for. In an environment filled with criminals and known conmen, their above-board approach had strong appeal. "I think the reason that everyone accepted NASCAR right from the beginning was because Bill and all of us made an honest effort not to line our own pockets," Tuthill added. "Our point fund was administered with honesty and integrity, too. I know it was Bill France's nature, and it was mine, to keep it completely honest."

At the awards dinner at the end of 1948, Tuthill claimed to have emphasized that point by standing up with a handful of checks and pointedly distributing them to the drivers, a policy that is still followed. Fielden said France meted out the checks. Regardless, it was not only unusual for drivers to receive money after a season, but they also realized they would get paid. As a result, competitors began arriving in NASCAR events from around the country.

"There was no question," Neely wrote, "NASCAR was there to stay."

The *NASCAR Media Guide* added, "The first decade for the NASCAR Winston Cup was one of tremendous growth. Characters became heroes, and fans hung on every turn of the wheel, watching drivers manhandle cars at speeds fans wish they legally could run themselves."

That's not an exaggeration. In 1948, the organization sanctioned 85 races. In 1949, the total jumped to 394. By 1951, there were more than 1,000 races carrying the NASCAR label. Drivers were beginning to discover the pot of gold waiting in Victory Lane.

The first official NASCAR beach race took place February 14, 1948, two days after NASCAR was officially incorporated. The event inaugurated Speedweeks, the annual two-week speed festival that now kicks off racing in this country. It wouldn't actually get christened with the Speedweeks tag until the following year. France naturally thought it up as part of a promotion. He also called the series of track activities "the Kentucky Derby of Auto Racing."

With the creation of NASCAR and the birth of Speedweeks, Daytona retained its cachet as the homeland of motorsports.

Naturally, there was a beach race that first year, offering its usual flurry of confusion and chaos. *Illustrated Speedway News* provided this description: "Ralph Sheeler was the first to miss the dangerous approach to the South Turn and go spilling over the edge of the back into the sand dune 12 feet below. Tex Callahan smashed up on the eighth lap in the identical spot and landed kerplung [*sic*] atop Sheeler's car."

Fireball Roberts overturned. Jack Ethridge ended up clinging to the rim of the South Turn, while Turk Atkins bashed into the already disabled cars. Fonty Flock lost a wheel and somersaulted unhurt into the palmettos. Only 10 cars actually finished the race.

Marshall Teague, who started on the pole after a drawing, ran all 150 miles without stopping for gas—the result of carrying an extra fuel tank in his back seat—but couldn't hold off Byron, who easily won his third straight race. Byron would go on to win the first NASCAR championship in what was called the Modified Division in 1948. The next year, it was titled "Strictly Stock." Later, the name would be changed to the Grand National Division, a moniker borrowed from motorcycle racing. In 1972 the series became known as the NASCAR Winston Cup Series, and, in 2004, the name became the NASCAR NEXTEL Cup Series.

As new tracks opened around the country, starting with Darlington Raceway, the sand at Daytona Beach became increasingly unusual and always challenging. "The old beach road track was wild and exciting," Tucker reported. "Sometimes cars would hit each other and tumble over the turns in crumpled heaps. Sometimes the beach would be wide and fast, sometimes rutted and narrow as incoming tides threatened. Spectators would park on the dunes and watch as race cars flew past, scant yards away."

To cope with the sprays from the surf, cars were equipped with windshield wipers. That came into play in 1958, the last year of beach racing. Although his wipers were no longer working, Paul Goldsmith opened up a large lead and calmly waved to his mechanic as he headed toward the final turn. He was looking through a hole in his windshield drilled by his mechanic to aid visibility. Long-time racer Marvin Panch said many mechanics used glass drills to create the holes, because visibility was often so poor.

The hole didn't help when Goldsmith hit some water while trying to avoid slower cars. The spray blinded him, and he sailed past the North Turn. Goldsmith, a former Indianapolis 500 racer, realized his mistake, braked and executed an abrupt

CE LAP OF FIRST "500" AT DARLINGTON SPEEDWAY

LABOR DAY - 1950

.. GOBER SOSEBEE - JIMMY THOMPSON - CURTIS TURNER

— FIRST ROW —

U-turn. With sand flying from spinning tires, he scrambled back onto the course. He ended up edging Curtis Turner by a few yards at the finish line.

Many cars bore screens over their front grille to block sand from choking their engines. The hairpin turns typically were glutted, as six or seven cars, some three or four wide, tried to career through an area not broad enough to hold two cars. One or two invariably went "out of the ballpark," skittering across the dunes and turning over in the sand. Doors were strapped shut with a belt or rope. Surplus army safety belts worked for drivers. Heads were protected by old British dispatch helmets or football gear.

In the bumping, grinding races, cars regularly lost wheels, suffered broken axles and shattered shocks. A local dealer might bring a car, hire a driver and, when the race was over, offer the car for sale in a used-car lot.

Cheating was commonplace. "The drivers didn't start the cheating," Tuthill insisted, "the factories did. The factory cars had all sorts of innovations, from disappearing fan belts to extra engine blocks in trunks for added weight." Chrysler used aluminum roll bars, lightened bodies and trick tires. Hudson tried putting a Hudson Wasp head backwards on a Hornet, which increased compression, but the engines often blew up. Oldsmobile altered its suspension.

As a result, a checkered flag didn't always reflect who officially won. Tim Flock crossed the finish line first in 1954, but was disqualified for using soldered carburetor butterflies. He got the trophy a year later when Fireball Roberts was disqualified for competing with altered push rods. Bob Flock was disqualified twice.

Superspeedways became part of NASCAR in 1950 at Darlington (South Carolina) Raceway with the first Southern 500. Curtis Turner, (No. 41) sat on the pole behind the pace car. Next to him was Jimmy Thompson (No. 25) with Gober Sosebee (No. 51) on the outside. Motorsports Images & Archives Photo

REMEMBERING THE OLD TRACKS

These days, NASCAR NEXTEL Cup drivers compete typically on ultramodern, paved facilities in front of thousands of fans. Daytona International Speedway, extending 2.5 miles, is one of the longest in NASCAR, exceeded only by Talladega Superspeedway. Most of the tracks are at least one mile around, but a few, like Richmond International Raceway and Bristol Motor Speedway, harken back to the early years when tracks usually were half a mile in length.

Then, drivers were happy to find any place to compete. On occasion, abandoned airstrips would be appropriated. Sometimes, drivers competed on boards. In Chicago, Soldier Field, a football stadium, was turned into a track. Early tracks were often fairgrounds or open fields where the dirt tossed up by the speeding cars would create an enveloping haze. In 1956, Lee Petty clamored from his car in a race at the Arizona State Fairgrounds and, disgusted by the relentless dirt, red-flagged the race.

After NASCAR began sanctioning races in 1948, the situation gradually began to improve. Tracks were being built around the country. The newer ones were often paved, adding to speed and improve visibility.

Here is a partial list by state of some of the bygone tracks that once hosted Grand National Division races, including name, length, surface and last year it was used.

State	Length	Surface	Last Year of Use
Alabama			
Alabama State Fairgrounds	.5 mile	dirt	1961
Birmingham Speedway	.5 mile	dirt	1968
Chisholm Speedway	.5 mile	dirt	1956
Dixie Speedway	.25 mile	paved	1960
Fairgrounds Speedway	.5 mile	dirt	1958
Huntsville Speedway	.25 mile	paved	1962
Lakeview Speedway	.75 mile	dirt	1951
Montgomery Motor Speedway	.5 mile	dirt	1968
Arizona			
Arizona State Fairgrounds	1 mile	dirt	1960
Tucson Rodeo Grounds	.5 mile	dirt	1955
Arkansas			
Memphis-Arkansas Speedway	1.5 mile	dirt	1957
California			
Ascot Stadium	.4 mile	dirt	1959
Ascot Speedway	.5 mile	dirt	1961
Bay Meadows Speedway	1 mile	dirt	1956
Capitol Speedway	.5 mile	dirt	1957
Carrell Speedway	.5 mile	dirt	1954
Eureka Speedway	.625 mile	dirt	1957
Hanford Motor Speedway	.5 mile	dirt	1951

State	Length	Surface	Last Year of Use
Los Angeles Fairgrounds	.5 mile	dirt	1957
Marchibanks Speedway	1.4 mile	paved	1961
Merced Fairgrounds	.5 mile	dirt	1956
Oakland Speedway	.625 mile	paved	1951
Ontario Motor Speedway	2.5 mile	paved	1980
Redwood Speedway	.625 mile	dirt	1956
Riverside International Raceway	.2631 mile	paved	1988
Sacramento Fairgrounds	1 mile	dirt	1961
Santa Clara Fairgrounds	.5 mile	dirt	1957
Willow Springs International Raceway	2.5 mile	dirt	1956
Connecticut			
New Thompson Speedway	.625 mile	paved	1969
Thompson Speedway	.5 mile	paved	1970
Florida			
Beach-Road Course	4.15 mile	sand	1958
Five Flags Speedway	.5 mile	dirt	1953
Golden Gate Speedway	.3 mile	dirt	1962
Palm Beach Speedway	.5 mile	dirt	1956
Speedway Park	.5 mile	dirt	1963
Georgia			
Augusta Speedway	.5 mile	dirt	1969
Augusta International Speedway	3 mile	paved	1963
Central City Speedway	.5 mile	dirt	1954
Columbus Speedway	.5 mile	dirt	1951
Hayloft Speedway	.5 mile	dirt	1952
Jeffco Speedway	.5 mile	paved	1969
Lakewood Speedway	1 mile	dirt	1959
Middle Georgia Raceway	.5 mile	paved	1967
Oglethorpe Speedway	.5 mile	dirt	1955
Savannah Speedway	.5 mile	dirt	1970
Valdosta "75" Speedway	.5 mile	dirt	1965
Illinois			
Santa Fe Speedway	.5 mile	dirt	1954
Soldier Field	.5 mile	paved	1956
Indiana			
Funk's Speedway	.5 mile	oiled dirt	1950
Playland Park Speedway	.5 mile	dirt	1952
Iowa			
Davenport Speedway	.5 mile	dirt	1953
Kentucky			
Corbin Speedway	.5 mile	dirt	1954

State	Length	Surface	Last Year of Use
Louisiana			
Louisiana Fairgrounds	.5 mile	dirt	1953
Maine			
Oxford Plains Speedway	.333 mile	paved	1968
Maryland			
Beltsville Speedway	.5 mile	paved	1970
Massachusetts			
Norwood Arena	.25 mile	paved	1961
Michigan			
Grand River Speedrome	.5 mile	dirt	1954
Michigan Fairgrounds	1 mile	dirt	1952
Monroe Speedway	.5 mile	dirt	1952
Nebraska			
Lincoln City Fairgrounds	.5 mile	dirt	1953
Nevada			
Las Vegas Park Speedway	1 mile	dirt	1955
New Jersey			
Linden Airport	2 mile	paved	1954
Morristown Speedway	.5 mile	dirt	1955
New Jersey State Fairgrounds	1 mile	paved	1972
Old Bridge Stadium	.5 mile	paved	1965
Trenton International Speedway	.5 mile	dirt	1900
Wall Stadium	.333 mile	paved	1958
New York			
Airborne Speedway	.5 mile	dirt	1955
Albany-Saratoga Speedway	.362 mile	paved	1971
Altamont Speedway	.5 mile	dirt	1955
Altamont-Schenectady Fairgrounds	.5 mile	dirt	1955
Bridgehampton Speedway	2.85 mile	paved	1951
Civic Stadium	.25 mile	paved	1958
Fonda Speedway	.5 mile	dirt	1968
Hamburg Fairgrounds	.5 mile	dirt	1950
Islip Speedway	.2 mile	paved	1971
Monroe County Fairgrounds	.5 mile	dirt	1958
Montgomery Air Force Base	2 mile	paved	1960
New York State fairgrounds	1 mile	dirt	1957
Shangri-La Speedway	.5 mile	paved	1952
State Line Speedway	.333 mile	dirt	1958
Vernon Fairgrounds	.5 mile	dirt	1950

State	Length	Surface	Last Year of Use
North Carolina			
Asheville-Weaverville Speedway	.5 mile	dirt	1969
Bowman-Gray Stadium	.25 mile	paved	1971
Central Carolina Fairgrounds	.333 mile	dirt	1958
Champion Speedway	.333 mile	paved	1958
Charlotte Fairgrounds	.5 mile	dirt	1960
Charlotte Speedway	.75 mile	dirt	1956
Cleveland County Fairgrounds	.5 mile	dirt	1965
Concord Speedway	.5 mile	dirt	1964
Dog Track Speedway	.25 mile	dirt	1966
Forsyth County fairgrounds	.5 mile	dirt	1955
Gastonia Fairgrounds	.333 mile	dirt	1958
Greensboro Agricultural Fairgrounds	.333 mile	dirt	1957
Harnett Speedway	.5 mile	dirt	1953
Harris Speedway	.3 mile	paved	1953
Hickory Speedway	.363 mile	paved	1971
Hub City Speedway	.5 mile	dirt	1962
Jacksonville Speedway	.5 mile	dirt	1964
McCormick Field	.25 mile	paved	1958
New Asheville Speedway	.4 mile	paved	1971
North Wilksboro Speedway	.05 mile	dirt	1957
North Wilksboro Speedway	.625 mile	paved	1996
Occoneechee Speedway	1 mile	dirt	1953
Orange Speedway	1 mile	dirt	1968
Raleigh Speedway	1 mile	paved	1958
Salisbury Super Speedway	.625 mile	dirt	1958
Starlite Speedway	.5 mile	dirt	1966
State Fairgrounds	.5 mile	dirt	1970
Tar Heel Speedway	.25 mile	dirt	1963
Tri-City Speedway	.5 mile	dirt	1954
Wilson County Speedway	.5 mile	dirt	1960
Ohio			
Bainbridge Fairgrounds	1 mile	dirt	1951
Canfield Motor Speedway	.5 mile	dirt	1952
Dayton Speedway	.5 mile	dirt	1952
Ft. Miami Speedway	.5 mile	dirt	1952
Powell Motor Speedway	.5 mile	dirt	1953
Oklahoma			
Oklahoma State Fairgrounds	.5 mil	dirt	1956
Oregon			
Portland Speedway	.5 mile	paved	1957
Pennsylvania			
Bloomsburg Fairgrounds	.5 mile	dirt	1953
Heidelberg Speedway	.5 mile	dirt	1960
Heidelberg Raceway	.25 mile	dirt	1959
Langhorne Speedway	1 mile	dirt	1957
Lincoln Speedway	.5 mile	dirt	1965
New Bradford Speedway	.333 mile	dirt	1958
Pine Grove Speedway	.5 mile	dirt	1951

State	Length	Surface	Last Year of Use
Reading Fairgrounds	.5 mile	dirt	1959
Sharon Speedway	.5 mile	dirt	1954
Williams Grove Speedway	.5 mile	dirt	1954

South Carolina

State	Length	Surface	Last Year of Use
Coastal Speedway	.5 mile	dirt	1957
Columbia Speedway	.5 mile	paved	1971
Gamecock Speedway	.25 mile	dirt	1960
Greenville–Pickens Speedway	.5 mil	paved	1971
Hartsville Speedway	.333 mile	dirt	1961
Lancaster Speedway	.5 mile	dirt	1957
Newberry Speedway	.5 mile	dirt	1957
Piedmont Interstate Fairgrounds	.5 mile	dirt	1966
Rambi Race Track	.5 mile	dirt	1965

South Dakota

State	Length	Surface	Last Year of Use
Rapid Valley Speedway	.5 mile	dirt	1953

Tennessee

State	Length	Surface	Last Year of Use
Boyd Speedway	.333 mile	paved	1962
Chattanooga International Raceway	.333 mile	paved	1964
Fairgrounds Speedway	.596 mile	paved	1984
Kingsport Speedway	.4 mile	paved	1964
Newport Speedway	.5 mile	dirt	1957
Smokey Mountain Raceway	.520 mile	paved	1971
Tennessee–Carolina Speedway	.5 mile	dirt	1956

Texas

State	Length	Surface	Last Year of Use
Meyer Speedway	.5 mile	paved	1971
(old) Texas International Speedway	2 mile	paved	1969

State	Length	Surface	Last Year of Use
Texas World Speedway	2 miles	paved	1981

Virginia

State	Length	Surface	Last Year of Use
Langley Field Speedway	.4 mile	dirt	1970
Norfolk Speedway	.4 mile	dirt	1957
Old Dominion Speedway	.375 mile	paved	1966
Princess Anne Speedway	.5 mile	dirt	1953
Roanoke Raceway	.25 mile	paved	1964
South Boston Speedway	.25 mile	paved	1971
Southside Speedway	.025 mile	paved	1963
Starkey Speedway	.25 mile	paved	1961

Washington

State	Length	Surface	Last Year of Use
Kitsap County Airport	.9 mile	paved	1958

West Virginia

State	Length	Surface	Last Year of Use
International Raceway Park	.437 mile	paved	1971
West Virginia International Speedway	.375 mile	paved	1964

Wisconsin

State	Length	Surface	Last Year of Use
Road America	4.1 mile	paved	1956

Canada

State	Length	Surface	Last Year of Use
Canadian National Exposition Speedway	.333 mile	paved	1958
Stamford Park	.5 mile	dirt	1952

Here are the modern tracks that NASCAR NEXTEL Cup drivers visit every year:

Name Location	Year Opened	Length
Atlanta (Ga.) Motor Speedway	1960	1.54 mile oval
Bristol (Tenn.) Motor Speedway	1961	.535 mil oval
California (Calif.) Speedway	1997	2 mile oval
(Charlotte) Lowe's (N.C.) Motor Speedway	1960	1.5 mile oval
Chicagoland (Ill.) Speedway	2001	1.5 mile trioval
Darlington (S.C.) Raceway	1950	1.366 mile oval
Daytona (Fla.) International Speedway	1959	2.5 mile trioval
Dover (Del.) International Speedway	1969	1 mile oval
Homestead-Miami (Fla.) Speedway	1995	1.5 mile oval
Indianapolis (Ind.) Motor Speedway	1909	2.5 mile oval
Kansas (Kan.) Speedway	2001	1.5 mile trioval
Las Vegas (Nev.) Motor Speedway	1996	1.5 mile oval
Martinsville (Va.) Speedway	1947	.526 mile oval
Michigan (Mich.) International Speedway	1968	2 mile oval
New Hampshire (N.H.) International Speedway	1990	1.058 mile oval
North Carolina (N.C.) Speedway	1965	1.017 mile oval
Phoenix (Ariz.) International Raceway	1964	1 mile oval
Pocono (Pa.) Raceway	1968	2.5 mile oval
Richmond (Va.) Raceway	1946	.75 mile oval
Infineon (Calif.) Raceway	1968	1.949 mile road course
Talladega (Ala.) Superspeedway	1969	2.66 mile trioval
Texas (Tex.) Motor Speedway	1997	1.5 mile oval
Watkins Glen (N.Y.) International	1956	2.45 mile road course

In 1950, after his first career win, Fireball Roberts (center) poses with wife, Doris, and car owner, Sam Rice. The victory at Occoneechee Speedway in North Carolina was not enough for the Florida native to finish ahead of Bill Rexford in the final standings. It was also Roberts's sole victory of the year and his only one for six years.
Motorsports Images & Archives Photo

Byron won one race despite having to use his emergency brake to slow when his brakes failed and having a coat hanger replace a broken shifter arm.

"It was wild and woolly," Tucker added.

It was crazy off the track, too. Photos show throngs filling a tall grandstand overlooking the North Turn while thousands of people and cars clogged the infield. Along the beach, another row of spectators sat and watched in or around their cars, ready to flee as soon as the tide rolled back in. Here and there, France posted "Beware of Rattlesnakes" signs along the overgrown dunes in a vain attempt to reduce the number of nonpaying spectators.

People tried to smuggle in nonpaying companions in trunks of cars. In one instance, a pilot landed a plane on the beach. Lunch in hand, he and his passengers wandered down to the track to watch the race. The high-tide area located north of the South Turn was reserved for the pit crews. Spectator parking filled the rest of the space to the North Turn. "Even with cars in two or three rows, fender to fender, the space couldn't accommodate all who wanted to be there," "Crawfish" Crider recalled.

The action was explosive. Everyone was looking for more speed. "If you don't stomp on the gas pedal, it's no fun driving," Bob Flock said.

Starting in 1949, the drivers reverted to the longer circuit originally thought best for only motorcycles. The shorter layout was simply too slow. The actual distance they drove really depended on the tide, which regularly altered the course. The track was measured at various times at distances from 4.1 to 4.3 miles.

The added straightaways still weren't fast enough for some drivers. In 1949, speed racing made a comeback on the beach. It began as impromptu competitions between young drivers showing off their cars and turned into a more formal event. The city provided some of the needed funding, while Tuthill and France recruited top dragsters. The city had no options. When NASCAR took control of the beach drag races, some of the drivers objected to a more rigid structure and relocated to Main Street, a beachside roadway better known for its connection to motorcycles. Efforts by police to stop them ended up in a near riot.

For drivers who only wanted the experience of speeding down the sand, France printed up certificates that verified an entrant had driven on the "World's Most Famous Beach." Other drivers competed against the clock and got a certificate for averaging 100 mph or higher. To ensure accuracy, the timer had to be retrieved from the Salt Flats in Utah. "There was only one around at the time," France explained. The timer was recalibrated, and the news trumpeted that the "world-famous Daytona timer was back in operation," he said.

In 1951, France induced Don Bailey, who had sped 208.972 mph on the Bonneville Salt Flats in Utah, to test the beach, reviving the memories of Campbell and other speedracers. Bailey, 23, revved up a Xydias-Batchelor So-Cal Special on February 8, 1951. The car, which resembled a "vacuum cleaner without the handle," according to Fielden, easily topped 200 mph, but then crashed. Bailey ended up in the hospital, marking the end of record attempts on the hard, uneven sand.

Drag racers, however, were not concerned. Until 1959, the speed races continued in several divisions, including modified cars, roadsters and convertibles. They raced on the beach or, from 1956-1959, at the Spruce Creek Airport, located in nearby Port Orange. The raucous action cemented Daytona Beach's reputation and helped NASCAR become the dominant sanctioning body in all of motorsports.

France brought the same diversity into his stock car racing. Most drivers drove modifieds— cars that had been "souped up" to compete in races. He created a Strictly Stock Division and added a Sportsmen's Division (later Sportsman). The Strictly Stock consisted of cars that could be driven directly off the showroom floor, while Sportmen's was designed for inexperienced drivers who wanted to get into racing at a lower price level. The Sportsmen's cars looked like modifieds, but their engines were missing dual carburetors and racing heads. They were wildly popular. As many as 118 cars competed in a single event. Usually, Modified and Sportmen's cars raced at the same time with winners declared in each division.

The Sportsmen's Division is also responsible for the introduction of radios in cars. Driver Al Stevens owned a wrecking service that relied on radios. On a whim, he put one in his car and connected it with his pits. He also placed two spotters along the track and gave them radios. For all his innovation, he finished 27th place. The original radio now sits in ISC Archives. Made by Motorola, it looks like a telephone on a wooden box, heavy and bulky.

The first Sportsmen's race in Daytona took place in 1952 with William Clifton France, the son of NASCAR's owner, getting his initial taste of local competition.

By the mid-1950s, Speedweeks had become such a massive promotion that other communities began to make pitches for it. Citing their ample size and large numbers of guest rooms, West Palm Beach and Miami fruitlessly, but relentlessly wooed

France. They had some history on their side. In 1926, Carl Fisher, who created the Indianapolis Motor Speedway, developed a track in Fulford-by-the-Sea, about 10 miles north of Miami. The 1.5-mile track was to become the foremost facility in the state and had hosted one race before a strong storm, probably a hurricane, demolished it. France listened to the various solicitations, but remained committed to Daytona Beach.

The races continued. Despite the rough-and-tumble driving, and the hardened men who competed, the first fatality didn't occur until 1954. Pennsylvanian Dick Kaufman, 23, lost a wheel on his 1949 Olds near the North Turn in a February Modified-Sportsman race and was killed in the resulting crash. A year later, Floridian Al Briggs, 33, was killed when his crippled car was hit and burst into flames.

The deaths helped motivate the American Manufacturers Association, which represented all car builders, to vote in 1957 to suspend all participation in car racing. The organization acted after a rash of fatalities on race tracks and highways. General Motors, Ford and Chrysler, which had seen sales peak after a racing victory by one of their cars, began to run tests and supply parts on the sly. The ban was quickly forgotten when the new season cranked up. Public interest was too high.

Much of it focused on the strange, increasingly outdated beach races. "The final decade of beach-road racing brought stock cars from rags to riches," Tuthill said. "It was a time of fun, excitement and fond memories. It was an unusual course that bred unusual happenings. It changed from year to year due to the action of the wind and tides, often from lap to lap because of the pounding of a stampede of race cars."

By 1958, however, time and tide were running out on the old course. Too many people lived nearby. Homes had been built where there had been curves in the paved highway. Tides often came in so fast that spectators found their cars swamped. That problem became acute in 1952, when the race had to be abbreviated when the tide rushed in sooner than expected.

And, as men like Campbell and Segrave realized long before, higher speeds created increasingly dangerous situations on the uneven surface.

Nor was there sufficient cash for massive improvements. There was no way to get every spectator to pay, not with miles of unfenced beach.

With Goldsmith's last-lap swerve to victory in front of an estimated 35,000 fans, beach racing came to its final pit stop. "The beach-road era had ended under a cold, gray sky," Fielden wrote. "There was no picturesque sunset on February 23, 1958. Darkness fell rapidly over the palmetto bushes. The tide rolled across the hard sands which only hours before had been the stage for an electrifying finish to one of the boldest chapters in stock-car racing history."

Daytona Beach Morning Journal sports editor Bernard Kahn, a pioneer in reporting on motorsports and whose name graces the media center at Daytona International Speedway, mourned it as "an old gal" who was "a ragamuffin" compared to the other famous tracks in the world.

Attention would shift to a 446-acre site about nine miles west of the beach, an area that was largely a swamp filled with pine trees and palmetto shrubs. Bill France would have about 10 months to turn the land located between a dog track and the city airport into a race track.

While he was working out the logistics, motorcyclists were still enjoying their turn on the beach. Unlike stock cars, motorcycles didn't resume racing in Daytona Beach in 1946. Manufacturers told the AMA there simply weren't enough riders to hold a national competition.

Fans and racers made their triumphant return to Daytona Beach in 1947. A record crowd estimated at 27,500 watched a record 142 entries take

Running alongside the Atlantic Ocean, 57 cars in the 1953 race on the sands of Daytona Beach line up in preparation for the green flag. Motorsports Images & Archives Photo

the green flag. Bikers battled each other and a brush-fire in the opening laps, with 1937 winner Ed Kretz dueling with Floyd Emde at first. Both bikes eventually broke, and Johnny Spiegelhoff rode in from Milwaukee, Wisconsin to win aboard an Indian.

The following year saw 153 entrants tackle the new 4.1-mile circuit. Emde prevailed despite a valiant late-race challenge by Billy Mathews, giving the Indian its second straight victory.

Mathews finished second the following year, with Norton rider Dick Klamforth scoring the victory. Mathews reversed that finishing order in 1950, but Klamforth rebounded with back-to-back triumphs the following two years. The 1952 race was delayed a day by rain, high winds and cold temperatures.

Harley-Davidson rider Paul Goldsmith gave the American marquee its first Daytona 200 victory in 13 years in the 1953 classic. Goldsmith, a future NASCAR Winston Cup star, averaged 94 mph. Two years later, Goldsmith was in contention to win when oil sprayed on his goggles, sending him into the ocean where a wave knocked him off his bike.

The next back-to-back winner on the sand was Joe Leonard, a future Indy Car champion, who triumphed in both 1957 and 1958. The latter race

ranked as one of the most one-sided in the history of the event, with Leonard's Harley blazing to victory in 99.86 mph, a beach record that would never be broken.

The same real estate development—coupled with deteriorating conditions on the road portion of the course—that forced France to find a new site for stock car races threatened the motorcycle events, too.

Still, the Daytona 200 managed to run on the sand through 1960. Brad Andres, won as a rookie in 1955, halting Leonard's streak in 1959, and backed it up by repeating in 1960. The latter event was the final race to be held on the sands of Daytona Beach and was staged by famed California promoter J.C. Agajanian.

While beachside competition was no longer possible, riders didn't have far to go to resume the Daytona 200. France's new superspeedway had already been hosting successful stock car races for two years. The AMA had been opposed to racing at the Speedway during its opening two years, fearing the high banks would be too fast for the motorcycles. For 1961, the organization had no other choice if the event was going to continue in Daytona Beach.

chapter nine

1959

Everyone seemed to agree that a superspeedway was the ideal replacement for the Beach-Road Course. They agreed on little else. From 1953 until the track opened in 1959, the idea was at the center of a series of missteps and confusing moves. Once it did open, the first Daytona 500 mirrored what had gone on before.

In 1953, the State Legislature approved creation of a Racing Authority to oversee development of a track. At the same time, Bill France formed the Daytona Beach Motor Speedway Corporation to build the facility—if he got the chance.

Lou Perini, then-owner of the Milwaukee Braves baseball team, showed up in December 1953 to look over sites and announced a willingness to invest $3 million in the project. By July 1954, he dropped the idea, convinced the highways serving Daytona Beach would never be able to handle all the traffic generated by the track. Anyone caught in the annual traffic jams these days can appreciate his foresight.

In January 1955, the Racing Authority, which consisted of six local community leaders, asked for bids from anyone interested in developing the site. France was the only person to respond.

On February 12, 1955, the Racing Authority accepted his bid. Two months later, the AAA announced it wouldn't sanction any cars that competed on the track if France were operating the track. No one paid much attention, since NASCAR was already sanctioning races around the region. Moreover, the AAA would drop out of racing two months later after

Bill France was all smiles in 1958, but he spent long hours raising money to fund the new speedway. It took five years to pay off the debt. Motorsports Images & Archives Photo

racer Bill Vukovich was killed at the 1955 Indianapolis 500. France immediately contacted the Federation Internationale de l'Automobile (FIA) to gain recognition for his series. As a result, NASCAR drivers can still compete in any international event and have driven in the Rolex 24 At Daytona, 24 Hours of Le Mans, the 12 Hours of Sebring, among other prestigious races.

In June 1955, the Civil Aeronautic Authorities (later renamed the Federal Aviation Administration) objected to the construction of a track because of radio transmissions and runways at the adjoining airport, now called Daytona Beach International Airport. The CAA wouldn't give final approval until December 1955.

The land also held concrete fuel-storage shelters used during World War II. So, the federal Department of Defense had to sign off on use of the land. That red tape was cut in October 1955.

On October 18, 1955, the *Daytona Beach Morning Journal* reported that the

city had approved a lease with the Speedway District for 377 acres of airport property.

France predicted the track would cost about $2.5 million and be ready by 1957. He was only off by two years and a lot of money.

The delay came from problems in the bond market. School and highway bond issues—the initial effects of the postwar "Baby Boom" and President Dwight Eisenhower's push for an upgraded highway system—shoved interest rates too high for the speedway. Attempts to locate funding stretched on for years. Finally, the Racing Authority (soon to be titled the Speedway District) called for a public referendum on the use of the land. The proposed vote, set for September 17, 1956, created enormous public debate with conflicting demands for a different date, support for the track and opposition to any development. The Authority eventually defused the uproar by announcing a delay in the vote and on October 30, 1956, reported a final agreement with Bill France to build the track.

The city had every reason to push the project. Preliminary estimates of economic impact from a single race totaled $1.8 million. In a community

A workman shovels dirt on the bottom of what became Lake Lloyd. Motorsports Images & Archives Photo

The girders for the grandstands created a maze. Today, the track holds 168,000 people. Motorsports Images & Archives Photo

totally dependent on tourism, that kind of jackpot overshadowed any other priorities.

In his formal announcement, France now estimated the speedway would cost $750,000 and have room for 10,000 spectators. He said the Daytona Beach Motor Speedway (quickly changed to Daytona International Speedway) would open on February 22, 1959, the anniversary of the birth of George Washington. He also expected to present a summer stock car race and a sports car event on a course to be built inside the speedway.

Finances remained a problem. France pre-sold tickets and used the money to pay for construction. "We still ended up owing a lot of money to various people, but we got it all paid off within five years after we opened the track," he said.

The big equipment needed to shove around 928,000 cubic yards of dirt was available because Clint Murchison Jr., a Texas developer, had run into problems with some of his projects in Cuba. Fidel Castro had launched a revolution on the island, located only 90 miles from

Florida, and threatened to shoot Murchison's men if they continued working on various sites there. On the other hand, General Fulgencio Batista, head of the faltering Cuban government and a part-time Daytona Beach resident, threatened to shoot the workers if they stopped construction. Caught in the middle, Murchison shipped his earth-moving equipment across the strait to Florida and started on the track. He also chipped in an estimated $500,000 loan to help fund the work and became the track's biggest stockholder. Eventually, about 1,200 mostly local residents owned shares in the new facility.

Some old-fashioned methods were also used to construct the track. Bill France Jr., who ran a grader, bulldozer and compactor once ground was broken in 1957, told *The News-Journal* that he once brought in a mule to help pull trees from a swampy

Paving equipment had to be held by thick chains to keep it from falling off the steep, 31-degree banks. Motorsports Images & Archives Photo

area of the land when machinery failed. "That didn't work either," he said. (He really is not Bill Jr. He has a different middle name than his father, but to avoid confusion, he has has been known as Bill Jr. his entire life.)

There were a few rattlesnakes to deal with, too. "The area was full of snakes," France recalled.

To complete the track, he said, "We went from 7 in the morning to 7 at night, and worked in the winter until it got dark."

Former Daytona Beach city engineer Charles Moneypenny was asked to design the Speedway. "I knew of no textbook on the subject of how to build a race track," he said. "When I began research on this track back in 1953, the first thing I learned was that most tracks are laid out by guesswork."

Reluctant to follow that haphazard pattern, Moneypenny gathered what information he could from other engineers and visited multiple race tracks. His expertise would eventually land him the job of designing Michigan International Speedway. His work also influenced the construction of California Speedway, which is based on the MIS blueprints.

France did have some specific plans for the new facility. He wanted two steeply banked turns "as steep as they could lay asphalt." That worked out to 31 degrees, created by dredging dirt from the infield and piling it up on the sides. The resulting 44-acre hole in the infield was filled in with water and dubbed Lake Lloyd, named for J. Saxton Lloyd, a local car dealer who was one of the original six members of the Speedway Authority and a significant contributor to the track's finances.

Visitors who take the track tour are usually stunned at how steep the banks really are. It's not as obvious to fans sitting in the stands or watching on television. Cars going too slowly will literally fall off them. France planned the banks to generate speed, akin to the way the turns on the old Beach-Road Course featured raised banks. The unusual feature, however, was not an homage to the old course. Indianapolis Motor Speedway was considered the fastest track in the country, and France wanted to surpass it.

He had a grudge against the historic track after being summarily escorted out of it less than five years earlier during time trials for the Indianapolis 500. The Associated Press account of the ejection said that AAA officials noted, "We have a longstanding disagreement with NASCAR on what constitutes good racing." France reportedly was good natured about the situation, saying he only wanted to shake hands with old friends and the "500 drivers, car owners and mechanics."

According to the *Daytona Beach Morning Journal*, France was ejected because the AAA, which sanctioned the Indianapolis 500, "considered him an unwanted intruder from NASCAR. With bulldog determination, France began mapping plans for a more modern and faster two and a half mile track than Indianapolis where he had been given a rude heave-ho."

He succeeded. Bill Elliott won the 1987 50-mile Busch Clash (now called the Budweiser Shootout At Daytona) at an average speed of 197.802 mph, setting a race-speed record still standing. Cars became so fast that, in 1988, NASCAR

Construction of the outer walls around the 2.5-mile track took months to complete. Motorsports Images & Archives Photo

was forced to require restrictor plates between the carburetor and the intake manifold, which cut fuel intake and reduced speeds at NASCAR's two high-speed tracks, Talladega Superspeedway and Daytona.

Generating speed was not the only thing on his mind. France also wanted spectators to be able to see at least one straightaway and one curve from any seat. That built on his beach-racing experience where he added a scoreboard and loud speakers to help spectators stay abreast of the action. To accomplish this goal, the track took on a D shape. France coined the word "trioval" to describe it.

The ability to view most of the race was considered an unusual feature for a large track. It's impossible to see the entire track in Indianapolis or at any road course, like Le Mans or Watkins Glen International. Today, sitting high up in any grandstand, a spectator can still clearly watch the complete race at Daytona International Speedway.

The track contains other features that made it an engineering marvel in 1959, including:

• 67,000 square yards of asphalt on the roadway

• 55,000 square yards of asphalt along the aprons, pits and grandstand

• Two galvanized steel tunnels, both 250 feet long and 14 feet in diameter, they are still the only way a car can get in and out of the track during a race.

• About seven miles of ditches for water drainage

• Concrete walls extending 3.5 feet high and 3,000 feet long to protect spectators; a 10-foot high safety fence tops the wall

• A chain-link fence stretching 14,000 feet long and 10 feet high around the entire track

• About 9,300 feet of extra-duty, ten-gauge steel used to support the guard rails, which are held in place by 1,500 posts placed at six-foot intervals

• Nine permanent grandstands, all named for famous racers, today, Daytona International Speedway can hold about 168,000 people in the grandstands and at least 75,000 more (no one counts) in the infield

• 25,000 extra-wide seats in the grandstands; Moneypenny insisted on the additional space, pointing out that people who would be sitting for up to four hours needed to be as comfortable as possible

To create that kind of facility, France had to scrounge up additional cash. Even family members pitched in. Bill Jr. was photographed working one of the graders. It wasn't a publicity shot.

Although not apparent at first glance, at one time the track featured five courses, based on the novel idea of nesting road courses inside the oval. The road courses vary in length from 3.8 to 1.3 miles, taking competitors through twisting turns in the infield before returning to the high banks. Daytona was the first track to do that and the first to give fans a view of an entire road course. A 100-yard chicane along the back straightway was added later and comes into play when sprint cars and motorcycles take off. Originally, motorcycles were not allowed on the high bank, but that changed in 1964 as upgraded engines produced sufficient speed.

The track was definitely fast. Fireball Roberts turned a test lap at 145.77 mph, almost reaching the record 148 mph posted at Indianapolis Motor Speedway. Reviving memories of his racing past, Bill France took a Pontiac convertible around the track at 114 mph.

"The only limit on speed is how fast the car will go and how fast you've got the nerve to drive it," said Roberts.

Not every driver was willing or able to shift from sand to asphalt. Hall of Fame driver Herb Thomas, who won two Grand National titles, was injured in 1956 and never raced at the Speedway. Buck Baker disliked superspeedways, but followed the series onto the high banks. Most of his 46 victories came on short tracks, however, although he notched checkered flags at Watkins Glen and Darlington (South Carolina) Raceway.

For others, the new track gave their careers a boost. Fireball Roberts spent much of his time on the beach courses skittering into sand dunes, but found his reckless style perfect for the Speedway. Curtis Turner, a former motorcycle champion named "Little" Joe Weatherly and ex-bootlegger Junior Johnson also came into their own when the sand was left behind.

At least one driver found that while the rewards were higher, so were the risks. In a practice run on February 10, 1959, Marshall Teague ran 171 mph in a Sumar Special Indy Car owned by Chapman Root Sr., a local busi-

During Speedway construction in 1958, chief engineer Charles Moneypenny (left) poses with Florida Governor Leroy Collins (center) and local businessman J. Saxon Lloyd. Lake Lloyd in the center of the infield is named for the late car dealer, who was a big booster of the track. Motorsports Images & Archives Photo

nessman whose family fortune was based on his father having designed the famous Coca-Cola bottle. The goal was to attain a speed of 180 mph.

Around noon on February 11, Teague drove down the front stretch on his third lap at a speed estimated at around 125 mph and waved to his pit crew. Before the second turn, the car started to slide and barrelrolled several times. Teague, one of the original participants in the meetings that founded NASCAR, was ejected from the car and was found 150 feet away, dead and still strapped into his seat.

The only Daytona Beach native to have won a beach race, Teague was also the first driver to obtain corporate sponsorship. Milford Brothers, a Hudson dealership in Jacksonville, loaned Marshall a new Hornet to race in 1951. The car was lettered in washable paint so it could be returned to the showroom if Teague did not win. After coming home first in the race, Teague joined with Bill France to convince Hudson and Pure Oil to sponsor the car. "Teaguemobiles" were put on display at Teague's Daytona Beach garage on Ballough Road at the foot of the Main Street Bridge. When Teague won the beach race again in 1952, interest zoomed. The Hudson teams eventually grew to 10 members and included Herb Thomas, Dick Rathman, Tim and Fonty Flock, Jack McGrath, Frank Mundy and Lou Figaro.

The loss of a star driver dampened spirits, as did the usual February rains. However, both enthusiasm and clouds cleared in time for the inaugural race weekend beginning February 21, 1959. No one knew what to expect. "The car that lasts, not necessarily the car that is fast, will win," the *Daytona Beach Morning Journal* opined.

Would anyone be there to see it? The beach crowds had burgeoned in recent years, but would they come to the Speedway? They did. Bill France was relieved. Gate receipts that weekend topped $500,000, but, as he noted to reporters, all of that money was owed to someone.

He did not schedule only a single race, but started with two 100-mile qualifiers, now known as the Gatorade 125s, and a modified race. Lloyd "Shorty" Rollins and Bob Welborn won the sprints. Rollins was forced to go to a backup engine, which he labeled as "junk," after his primary engine failed the day before.

On Saturday, February 22, Edwin "Banjo" Matthews won the inaugural 80-lap modified race before 17,000 people. His 1956 Ford with a 1959 Lincoln engine averaged 134.655 mph, giving a strong suggestion of what speeds drivers could expect the next day in the big race. Matthews won $2,400, which only partially covered the $4,000 he said was invested in the car.

For the first Daytona 500, a capacity crowd estimated at 47,000 turned out to watch 59 cars climb the high banks. Not everyone paid to get in. Some enterprising fans relied on the old "hide-in-the-trunk" trick. Hundreds of others slipped in through a trench dug under the fence across from the Keech Grandstand.

Cotton Owens qualified first at 143.198 mph. In contrast, Goldsmith won the pole for the last beach race with a clocking of 140.570 mph.

FLAGS

When the cars rolled down the front straightaway to begin the inaugural Daytona 500 in 1959, race officials used flags to communicate with drivers who were clocking at speeds up to 180 mph.

By then, flags had become the usual method of official communication. They have been part of racing for years and have links to a variety of sources. Ships at sea have long used flags to communicate across distances. The military has also relied on flags, dating back to ancient times. When trains started to rumble across the landscape, engineers also developed signal flags to send messages.

Green was used for go, while red became stop, later transferring to signal lights on streets.

Those same two colors and their meanings were picked up for racing.

Little else is known about early racing flags, if they existed at all. According to the Flags of the World (FOTW) website, flags were first used in motorsports in 1899, but only the red (stop) and the yellow (caution) flags. Other colors were added as situations arose that needed to be addressed.

The media tended to ignore the flags. No reports on the earliest of races, held in Europe or this country, indicate the use of flags. The same is true for drivers trying to set speed records in Daytona Beach. The stories consistently talk about a "signal" to go, which may be a flag or simply a timer holding up an arm.

Besides, the cars passed under a black-and-yellow sign indicating the start and end of the measured mile. No flags apparently were used.

At some point, however, flags showed up at the track. Versions in the United States and abroad are different. For example, American races start with a green flag; European Formula One races once began by waving the national flag of the country where the race was being held.

Over the years, the meanings of the various hues have changed.

Flags used in the 1936 beach race and today include:
GREEN—Start of race; course is clear
YELLOW—Caution; bring car under control, reduce speed
RED—Danger; stop
CHECKERED—Race over

Modern racers have three other flags to watch for:
BLACK—Pit immediately
BLUE with yellow stripe—Move over so faster car can pass
WHITE—Last lap

In 1936, these additional flags were in use, according to a *Daytona Beach Morning Journal* report.

ORANGE (with blue center)—Competitor is attempting to overtake you
WHITE—Report to your pit on the next lap
BLUE—Entering the last lap

The colors all seem plausible, except for one—the checkered flag. Why checkered? Use of it is definitely old. The earliest known mention of the unusual flag appears in a 1937 book by Fred J. Wagner, entitled—*A Story of Early Auto Racing in America*. A well-known race official, Wagner noted that in 1900 that, "I made my New York debut as an automobile starter at the old Empire City track and gave Barney (Oldfield) the checkered flag at the end of an unbelievably smashing mile race."

Checkered flags also appear in photos taken about 10 years after that 1900 reference.

Initially, checkered flags were reserved for the Indianapolis 500. However, in 1936, after trying unsuccessfully to buy a checkered flag, Mamie Thomas, the mother of early starter and car builder Frank Thomas, sewed one for the 1936 beach race in Daytona. That flag was used for many years before being added to the International Motorsports Hall of Fame in Talladega, Alabama, according to Frank Thomas, who spoke to the author in 2002. He was 87 at the time.

Chris Economaki, a long-time motorsports writer, editor and commentator, said the first checkered flag was a tablecloth hastily picked up and waved as an impromptu method to end a race in France prior to the start of the 20th century. But, how would the racers have known what it meant?

NASCAR archivist Buz McKim speculated that the black-and-white checks were sufficiently eye-catching and understandable for even a color-blind driver. That doesn't explain the red and green flags in regular use.

Naval flags include one that is checkered, but it signifies caution.

"Someone told me that they thought the origins of the flag lay in its use in bicycle races in France at the turn of the century," according to Ian Sumner, who posted his findings on the FOTW website. "Since the first Grand Prix proper was in France in 1907 under the auspices of the Automobile Club de France, this may be the case," he wrote, "but I have not found anything in books of motor racing history, nor in the FIA rule book or website, to back it up."

One thing at least is known about the checkered flag: Even if no one knows how it came into use, it remains the one flag every driver wants to get.

The first event on the new Daytona International Speedway in 1959 featured Modified cars.

Goldsmith's time was recorded on a straight run; Owens had to negotiate four turns.

Welborn, Weatherly and "Tiger" Tom Pistone swapped the lead for the first 22 laps. Fearful of going through the fence and ending up in Lake Lloyd, Pistone carried scuba gear in his car.

Hometown favorite Roberts then shot to the front. Welborn would not finish the race. He was not aware that his chief mechanic knew the engine had a fatal flaw in it and would eventually blow up. It did. There simply hadn't been enough time for a major repair.

Also competing was Richard Petty, the son of veteran Lee Petty. A famous photo from the beach races shows a slim teenager standing at the edge of the North Turn watching Lee Petty's car kick up sand in the last beach race. The youngster was Richard, getting pointers. He would drop out of the 1959 Daytona 500 early because of engine problems and finish 57th, but would return to win "The Great American Race" a record seven times.

In 1959, his father took the lead at the 375-lap mark in his No. 42 Olds 88. Then 44, Petty had the only Oldsmobile sedan in the race. He was challenged by Johnny Beauchamp in a No. 73 Ford Thunderbird. The two of them swapped the lead the rest of the way in what local sports editor Benny Kahn called a "blazing neck 'n' neck duel" in "the fastest, most spectacular 500-mile, late-model 'stock car' race ever run anywhere."

Many of the top competitors fell away, often brought to the pits by tire wear. While Beauchamp changed only one rear tire in four pit stops, Pistone was forced to get new tires nine times. Curtis Turner went through 12 sets of tires; so did Dewayne "Tiny" Lund. Manufacturers blamed style of driving, not the heat generated on the new track by the higher speeds. Only 33 of the original starters finished the race; five were on the lead lap.

Without a single caution to slow them down, Petty and Beauchamp stayed in front. They were eventually joined by Weatherly, who was a lap down and desperately trying to catch up. Beauchamp was on the inside, Petty in the middle and Weatherly on the outside as they charged three abreast toward the finish line. "They ran wheel to wheel through the high banks of the west turn and down the back straightaway. The three cars roared through Turns 3 and 4 as if they were welded together, not one of them giving an inch," historian Neely wrote.

Official starter John Bruner Sr., whose son was his assistant, couldn't tell who won because the waving checkered flag obscured his view. Reporters in the temporary press box thought Petty had triumphed by a foot or so. Bill France thought Beauchamp had finished first and called him the "unofficial temporary winner." Beauchamp and Petty both went to Victory Lane, although Petty left as soon as France made his tentative pronouncement.

"I'm confident I won," said Beauchamp, described as a "boyish-looking bachelor." The former IMCA champ had come from Iowa to drive in the NASCAR-sanctioned event. He said he took the outside line intentionally and had taken the lead. He also blamed Weatherly for "riding him rough."

Weatherly returned the favor by calling Petty the winner. "If Petty didn't win this race," Weatherly proclaimed, "he never won a race."

France took his time issuing a decision. Five hours after the race ended, and several hours after getting official photographs taken at the finish line, he finally announced that the final results could not be issued until later. Having endured years of bureaucratic holdups simply to build the track, the wily NASCAR president had learned a lot about publicity that accompanied delays.

While the media continued to suggest various scenarios, France dragged out the official report as long as possible, claiming to watch newsreels and inviting any spectator who took photos to come forward. Bob Torbal, a Duluth, Minnesota resident, showed up with a photo he took from the pits. While the cars are blurred, they do depict Weatherly, Petty and Beauchamp finishing in that order. In a race that lasted three hours, 44 minutes and 22 seconds, Petty managed to win by an estimated 18 inches. It may have been the closest finish ever in a race at that point and remains one of the tightest races in racing history.

After pondering the evidence for a total of 61 hours, France finally declared Petty the official winner. Interrupted at supper in his home in North Carolina with the news, Petty declined to head down to Daytona Beach immediately to receive the $19,000 first-place check. "I'm still eating my dinner, and I'm going to finish it," he commented. "This is a good piece of ham, and, man, I'm hungry."

His win helped cement a Hall of Fame career that included 54 wins and really ended in 1960 following an accident, although he ran a handful of races through 1964. Weatherly, who officially ended up fifth, would go on to become one of NASCAR's great drivers and give his name to the Hall of Fame in Darlington. Beauchamp was very disappointed by the results, but recovered to win a March race in 1959 and to drive for Petty later in the year. He would win only one other race in his career.

The track, however, had become the center of attention. NASCAR and Daytona Beach had brushed off the sand and found incredible luster beneath.

Four cars test Daytona International Speedway prior to its 1959 opening.
Motorsports Images & Archives Photo

With stands full, drivers roll down the short chute toward the first green flag in "The Great American Race." Motorsports Images & Archives Photo

chapter ten

1960-71

The close finish, the huge crowd and the publicity surrounding the 1959 Daytona 500 combined with Daytona's storied history to create an aura about the event, eventually elevating the race to a level approached only by the Indianapolis 500 in public interest and affection.

The added attention translated into bigger purses. Red Byron won only $5,800 in 1949 while winning the first championship. Fred Lorenzen topped the $100,000 mark with his 1963 title. In 1969, David Pearson banked more than $200,000. The $300,000 level was splintered two years later by Richard Petty, who then scaled the $400,000 barrier in 1974. Bill Elliott smashed the $1 million mark in 1985 with $2.38 million. In 1998, Jeff Gordon took home $9.3 million for his second straight NASCAR Winston Cup championship. In 2002, all regular competitors earned at least $1 million in prize money.

Modern drivers compete in the most aerodynamic, technically advanced stock cars available. In the 1960s, drivers wrestled with their vehicles as much as they steered. "The cars must have weighed 4,500 to 5,000 pounds," according to John Ervin, an International Motorsports Hall of Fame mechanic who worked for two-time champion Ned Jarrett. "With no power steering," he said, "you had to be really strong in your upper body to drive one of those things."

Initially, the cars were simply taken off a showroom floor, stripped of amenities, given a roll cage and heavier springs. In the 1960s, engineers devised a fabricated chassis, which reduced weight and added speed.

OPPOSITE: **Bill France wanted to outdo Indianapolis and ordered the high banks he's sitting on in the 1960s built as steep as possible. That came out to 31 degrees, allowing the stock cars eventually to hit speeds higher than the open-wheel cars of Indy. Later, NASCAR slowed the cars as a safety precaution.** Motorsports Images & Archives Photo

One element of racing stayed the same throughout the expansion in the 1960s—Bill France ran NASCAR, exercising tight control. As a result, the sanctioning body continued to prosper.

France's biggest hurdles were finding adequate tracks and deciding how many races to run. In 1949, Byron competed in only six races to claim the title. A year later, Bill Rexford made 17 starts to edge Fireball Roberts for the championship. In 1951, Herb Thomas finished atop the standings after 34 races. By 1956, the season consisted of 48 races. The number hit 50 in 1958, peaking at 62 in 1964. By 1973, the total had dropped to 28 and stabilized in the 30s thereafter. Today's racers compete in 36 races as well as an all-star race at Lowe's Motor Speedway and as many as two additional races during Speedweeks at Daytona—one of the two 125-mile Daytona 500 qualifying races and, if they won a pole in the previous year, the Budweiser Shootout at Daytona.

Tracks then and now are still scattered from Florida to Maine and as far west as California. Races over the years have been held in 34 different states, as well as in two cities in Canada. Tracks in the early years were often dirt and short, typically about one-half mile around. Paved, high-speed tracks were limited to Atlanta, Charlotte, Darlington and Daytona Beach until 1969 when Talladega Superspeedway in Alabama was added.

NASCAR drivers competed on dirt for the last time on September 30, 1970, a 100-mile race held on the State Fairgrounds in Raleigh, N.C.

Richard Petty posted an average speed of 68.376 mph and took home $1,000 along with the checkered flag.

Stock-car racing was still a regional sport, but it was on its way to national prominence, fueled by television that focused on charismatic drivers who developed their reputations at high speed. The years 1959 to 1972 represented an era of "fierce competition for small purses, when winning first place was the only thing that counted," Neely wrote. "It was the heyday of the hard-chargers. When the flag dropped, there was always a mad charge to the front."

The popular sports anthology, ABC's *Wide World of Sports*, included a small portion of the Firecracker 400 in a 1961 broadcast. From then on, snippets from races appeared in various television sports shows. Accounts of races began being reported widely, if usually only briefly, in newspapers around the country. In time, the names of Richard Petty, Bobby Allison, David Pearson, Buddy Baker, Ned Jarrett, Fred Lorenzen and others began to creep into the public consciousness.

No driver is more responsible for the rise of NASCAR in these turbulent years than Richard Petty, who soon garnered the nickname of "The King." Nobody has won more NASCAR Winston Cup races, 200, or come close—Pearson, in second place, trails by 95 victories. No one made a bigger commitment to the fans. Even on crutches and unable to drive because of an injury, Petty would sign autographs and greet spectators before and after races.

His sunglasses, southern drawl and trademark piano-keyboard smile became familiar icons to a generation of race fans. "He was the best ambassador stock car racing has ever had," Bill France said.

Petty achieved his prominence by closely observing the 1959 races at Daytona International Speedway and noticing a few racing anomalies that set his destiny.

For starters, he discovered that the outside groove was actually faster. "If (the other drivers) decided to run on the inside of the track, I decided I could go better on the outside," he explained. "My guess was as good as theirs. I formed a habit of running up high because I didn't have that much horsepower. This was the only way I could stay competitive, just run wide open all the way around the track and use the high banks to my advantage." In the 1962 Daytona 500, Petty ran laps up to eight mph slower than the eventual winner, Fireball Roberts, and still nearly got to the checkered flag first.

Also, the North Carolina native realized that cars passed but could not pull away. "I first noticed the effect when I was running off the banks to keep up with the pack," Petty said. "Every once in awhile, I would go whizzing right by them as if they had stopped. Then, a little later, they could come flying by me—the whole pack I had just blown off."

He began to experiment with driving techniques and discovered the "slingshot" effect. Only David in the Bible was more effective with a slingshot. Petty would wait until the final lap, then go high and roll through the second corner, picking up speed and passing the leaders. "I was actually catching their draft but didn't know it," he said. "The car shot around them into first place."

If he made his move too quickly, the other cars would catch his draft and pass him in the third turn.

Petty may have been the first to understand the drafting process, but his father, Beauchamp and Weatherly didn't need a rookie to tell them what to do in 1959. They were drafting through the last

Like many early NASCAR Winston Cup champions, Bobby Allison had a Southern background. Although a native of Florida, he became famous as the leader of the "Alabama Gang." Motorsports Images & Archives Photo

47 laps of the inaugural Daytona 500 without even being aware of the process.

The younger Petty had one other advantage: he had never raced on the huge trioval before, like everyone else, but he also rarely raced on short tracks. He had no bad habits to unlearn. "For once," Petty said, "not knowing anything was a blessing."

He would go on to create the records everyone else is still shooting at, including most championships (seven) and most career starts (1,177). He still holds the record of winning 10 straight races set in 1967. He won on short tracks, paved and dirt that year and added a superspeedway win in the Southern 500.

In 1967, Petty also set the record for the most short-track races won in succession (10). His streak started at Nashville International Raceway and ended with a second-place finish behind Bobby Allison by a car length at Asheville-Weaverville Speedway. Petty also set the record for the most consecutive short-track wins (six) in the same event, winning the spring race at North Wilkesboro Speedway from 1970 through 1975.

He had a chance to race against his father only briefly. In 1961, Lee, three-time NASCAR Strictly Stock champ, was hurt in an accident in a qualifying race at Daytona. On the last lap of a then-100-mile Daytona 500 qualifying race, the elder Petty tried to avoid a sliding Banjo Matthews and was rammed by Johnny Beauchamp. The cars locked bumpers and ended up sailing over the eastern wall. Badly injured, Lee Petty, who died in 2001, raced only a few times through 1964, then retired.

Richard was also caught up in a crash in the other 1961 qualifying race. In a three-car melee that included Junior Johnson and Fireball Roberts, Petty's No. 43 was sent through a guard rail, over the western wall and into the parking lot four stories below. He sprained an ankle stumbling from his car, but was otherwise unhurt.

The 1961 Daytona 500 went to Marvin Panch after Fireball Roberts' car lost its starter—it fell out of the car and punctured his oil pan—with 13 laps remaining and a one-lap lead. A year later, Roberts came back to win despite running out of gas twice. He thought the car would go 100 miles on a full tank; it only went 98. Roberts changed two right-side tires throughout the entire race and set a high standard that weekend by setting world records for 500 miles (152.529 mph); qualifying time (158.744 mph); and victories in the 250-mile pole position race (156.440) and a 100-mile qualifying race (156.999), along with his lone Daytona 500 triumph.

A superstitious man, as many drivers still are, Roberts worried throughout the entire 1962 Daytona 500 because Mary Ann Mobley, a former Miss America who was "Miss Speedweeks" that year, kissed him prior to the race. The only other time a woman kissed him before a race, Roberts had crashed. Mobley's buss "scared me to death," Roberts admitted.

"I acted impulsively, and just reached up and kissed him on the cheek for luck," said Mobley, who promptly apologized when she saw his expression.

Caught in a fiery 1964 crash in Charlotte, N.C., Roberts died in a hospital six weeks later. Joe Weatherly, the "crown prince" of racing, was killed on a track the same year. Their deaths led to added safety features, including lined fuel cells. The days when ropes served as safety belts were over. "Mad" Marion McDonald drove on the beach course with a knife on the dashboard to cut his rope belt in case of an emergency. By the mid-1960s, he wouldn't have been allowed in a car.

No one argued about the need for safety. The two areas of major contention in the 1960s were over unions and engines.

Curtis Turner initiated the union uproar. Once a partner of Bill France in a Mexican Road Race—where they were disqualified for shifting to another car—Turner started to run low on money in the early 1960s. He was building Charlotte (now Lowe's) Motor Speedway and obtained extra cash from the Teamsters Union. In exchange, Turner agreed to help organize the drivers. France squelched the effort by immediately suspending Turner, who would not be allowed to return to racing until 1965. A few protests by fans, more enamored with Turner's aggressive style than concern for labor unions, quickly faded.

In 1969, the Professional Drivers Association led by Richard Petty met with a similar tough stance. The PDA had been founded "to improve pit conditions and garage-area accommodations, and to assist drivers with endorsements and personal appearances." The impetus for a drivers' union had come from Larry LoPatin, a real-estate developer who built tracks in Michigan and Texas. He also had interest in tracks in Atlanta and Riverside, California. With the support of Ford Motor Co., LoPatin wanted to force France from NASCAR and either take over the sanctioning body or replace it, according to Kahn.

LoPatin found what he thought was the ideal site for a confrontation—Talladega Superspeedway. The track had been built "mainly to help us with our cash-flow problem in Daytona," France said. "We opened Talladega to promote events during non-race periods in Daytona." The new track featured steeper banks and higher speeds. LoPatin

Richard Petty's distinctive look invariably features a feathered cowboy hat and sunglasses.
Motorsports Images & Archives Photo

played up the dangers associated with the rapid pace. As a result, PDA members, who consisted of the most successful drivers, threatened to boycott the track over safety concerns.

France ran the race anyway with any competitors willing to strap on a helmet, including a lone "big name" driver, Bobby Isaac. France also borrowed a Ford and drove 176 mph around the track. "If a 60-year-old man can drive 176, surely our top drivers can do it safely at 20 miles over that," he said.

His exhibition punctured the argument. LoPatin's dream of a racing empire quickly faded into bankruptcy. The PDA lost any power. In 1973, Petty resigned as president; the union folded within a few months.

France shrugged off complaints from some drivers and the media that he was a czar. "I don't know what a czar is," he said. "If being a czar is owing a lot of money, then I'm a czar."

He then formed International Speedway Corporation as the holding company for the two tracks. The France family held 1.25 million shares in the new company; Union Oil held one million.

The skirmish with the PDA reflected a deep rift with Ford that began a decade earlier. In order to increase competitiveness, each car manufacturer had steadily boosted power. In 1962, Pontiac was turning out 465 horsepower in its 421-cubic-inch V-8. Dodge and Plymouth's Mopar engines offered a 413-cubic-inch engine while Chevrolet came in at 409 cubic inches. Ford lagged at 406 cubic inches. As a result, the company that had dominated beach

racing found itself trailing badly on speedways. High speeds simply cracked the Ford blocks.

In 1963, Ford countered by cross-bolting the main bearings. The results were favorable. Lund, substituting for an injured Melvin Panch, won the Daytona 500 that year in a Ford with Fred Lorenzen and Ned Jarrett, both in Fords, right behind. Lund ran out of gas crossing the finish line for the first of his five career wins. Lund, who was anything but a small man, had been given the ride the day before. Panch had crashed practicing a Maserati sports car 10 days prior to the Daytona 500, and Lund courageously helped pull the stricken driver from the burning car. From his hospital bed, Panch asked car owners Glen and Leonard Wood to let Lund race his car.

In 1964, Chrysler reacted to Ford's success by re-introducing the "Hemi," an updated version of the engine that had powered their entries on the beach. The engine featured a hemispherical combustion chamber, but it had been dropped in an economy move in the 1957 model. Ford tried to introduce a new 427-cubic-inch, single overhead camshaft engine, but France banned it as nonstock. Forced to use its old, noncompetitive engine, Ford languished all season.

Frustrated, Ford officials insisted that NASCAR sanction its new engine. Chrysler, of course, demanded that NASCAR leave everything as it was. France tried to broker an agreement, but winter meetings in Detroit met with no success. Ford's disappointment with NASCAR led to its involvement with LoPatin.

MONEY BAGS

When Dale Earnhardt won the 1998 Daytona 500, he set two records, one of which was obscure. Everyone realized that he had spent more futile years than any other competitor before winning "The Great American Race."

Most fans, however, were not aware that the North Carolina legend was the first driver ever to earn more than $1 million for his long-awaited visit to Gatorade Victory Lane.

Earnhardt took home $1,059,150. In contrast, Lee Petty, who won the inaugural Daytona 500 39 years earlier, received $19,500 for his razor-thin victory, the largest award offered to any winner in a NASCAR race that year.

In 2003, Ryan Newman, who ended up last in the Daytona 500, took home $173,788. His check still exceeded the purse for the entire field in the 1959 Daytona 500. That's been true for every driver who finished 43rd since 1998.

In 2003, the posted awards for the Daytona 500 totaled $13,816,240, an increase of $1.5 million from the previous year's total. Winner Michael Waltrip eventually pocketed about $1.4 million of that purse. Kurt Busch finished second and earned slightly more than $1 million.

That kind of reward helps drive the competitors.

"If the Daytona 500 didn't pay prize money, it would still be the race that every driver wanted to win," Jeff Gordon said in 1998, when the purse was less than half the 2004 total. "But, with $6 million on the line, it will give all of us even more incentive to race hard and put on a great show for the millions of people who watch the Daytona 500 each year."

Think what $14 million in incentive must do.

The big increase in the winner's share came in 1980 from $73,900 in 1979 to $102,175 then to $119,600 in 1983. Not coincidentally, television began to cover the Daytona 500 in 1979. The additional revenue made the boost in awards possible.

Ironically, the Daytona 500 has not always been the most lucrative NASCAR race. At one time, the biggest purse in NASCAR history, $4.965 million, was paid by the Indianapolis Motor Speedway for its 1997 Brickyard 400. Winner Ricky Rudd took home $571,000.

The Indianapolis track also paid out $8.6 million, then the biggest purse in racing history, for the 1999 Indianapolis 500, which features cars from the Indy Racing League. The Daytona 500 purse has now surpassed the Indianapolis payoff. In 2003, Indianapolis 500 winner Gil de Ferran earned $1,353,265 from a purse of $10.4 million.

The Daytona 500 payout is now larger. It dwarfs total purses at any other track. For example, purses offered at the next three races on the schedule—at North Carolina Speedway, Atlanta (Georgia) Motor Speedway and Las Vegas (Nevada) Motor Speedway—will not add up to the $15 million available to drivers in the 2004 Daytona 500.

The purse at Texas Motor Speedway is currently the second largest on the NASCAR NEXTEL Cup tour. It topped $6.1 million in 2003.

There's a good reason the most famous stock car race in the world offers the biggest purse.

"The Daytona 500 is the most prestigious race in the NASCAR NEXTEL Cup Series, and this year's competitors will be rewarded handsomely for their efforts," Daytona International Speedway President Robin Braig said.

Eventually, France also banned the Hemi because the racing engine was not available to the public. Chrysler promptly ended its relationship with NASCAR.

Without its prime competitor, Ford enjoyed a dominant 1965, including the top 10 finishers in the Daytona 500 that year. Anthony Joseph "A.J." Foyt, on his way to legendary status with four Indianapolis 500 wins, took home the 1965 Firecracker 400 trophy in a Ford. He was so confident of victory that he drove into the pits late in the race simply to ask his startled crew if anyone wanted to talk to him. He also won the 1972 Daytona 500, one day after openly predicting he would.

Buck Baker was a Southern racer who went on to achieve national prominence. Motorsports Images & Archives Photo

Chrysler began producing the Hemi for its passenger cars and returned to racing with the engine in late 1965. In response, Ford tried to introduce its single overhead cam engine again, only to be countered by NASCAR. Ford then followed Chrysler's lead and pulled out of NASCAR before being mollified by a compromise plan. France said he'd reconsider the Ford engine once enough of them had been produced for passenger cars.

The fighting between the manufacturers was typical—and nonstop. "Engine and chassis and body design changes were commonplace. It was a time when money seemed to be no object. Winning was everything," historian Neely reported.

"It seems like the drivers have grown up, but the manufacturers haven't," he quoted an unidentified "long-time NASCAR observer."

Inspections regularly turned up illegal modifications. "Everyone was caught in the whirlwind of change-or-run second syndrome."

The battles on and off the track between manufacturers simmered until 1970, when NASCAR briefly introduced restrictor plates for the first time to reduce speeds at Talladega. "In order to cut down on blown engines and tire wear, all of which was extremely expensive for our independent team," France announced, "we decided to slow down."

Predictably, the manufacturers disagreed. Dodge and Plymouth insisted the move was a plot to help Ford. Ford said the move was designed to lure back Chevrolet, which had dropped out of NASCAR after a tiff over its engines. Actually, Chevrolet would not return until 1973.

The racing went on regardless of the sniping. Fans came to see the drivers, men they grew to know well in these wild years when everything that could happen, did happen, on a track. Because of Daytona's place in racing, victories there were even more important, leading to a variety of strange, even surrealistic, events.

In 1965, the race was shortened by rain. Fred Lorenzen won it while sitting in the pits with a flat tire. It's a good thing the race could not resume; someone had stolen the checkered flag. In 1966, Richard Petty won a rain-shortened Daytona 500 by a full lap after many windshields were cracked by chunks of rubber torn off tires traveling more than 170 mph.

In 1968, William Caleb "Cale" Yarborough, a South Carolina tobacco farmer, won a crash-filled Daytona 500. A hole had to be cut in Yarborough's grille to get at trash that might block air to the radiator. There were so many accidents that the pace car overheated and had to be replaced. Driver Earl Brooks escaped one crash by climbing on the hood of his disabled car and holding onto the fence while other cars whizzed by.

In 1969, LeeRoy Yarbrough won the Firecracker 400 after adding a single soft-compound tire to his left rear wheel. The tire was good for 30 laps; he was 20 laps from the end when it was installed. The tire added just enough grip to get by Charlie Glotzbach.

In 1970, Plymouth introduced a "Superbird" which featured a raised rear spoiler. Pete Hamilton, a former rock-and-roll drummer, won the Daytona 500 that year in the odd-looking "winged thing," as one observer called it.

In 1971, Bobby Isaac won the Firecracker 400 while waiting for his hood to pop off. One by one, three of the four pins holding the hood in place let go. Wind was cutting under the loosened hood and lifting the car off the ground when the checkered flag finally waved.

A year later, Richard Petty and David Pearson alternated being on the point 50 times in the last 48 laps of the Firecracker 400. "It reminded me that I am too old for this sort of thing," said famed crew chief Leonard Wood. Pearson won by a few feet with Bobby Allison only inches behind Petty.

The race ended an era. Dirt tracks were gone. R.J. Reynolds Tobacco Company would begin corporate sponsorship of the series. NASCAR changed the name from "Grand National" to Win-

ston Cup and labeled 1972 the beginning of the "modern era."

In many ways it was. The old racers, the ones who had initiated the sport on the sands in Daytona Beach, created the rules and set the standards for speed and daring, were long retired. They had been replaced by competitors who were achieving national prominence. Besides Petty, who would retire in 1992, they included the following drivers:

Bobby Allison raced from 1961 to 1988. The leader of the Alabama Gang, a group of racers who made their homes in that state, Allison was originally from Florida. His wandering ways led him to drive for 23 teams in his career and in every series

Richard Petty became "The King" of NASCAR by rolling up 200 career wins and seven championships in racing's elite series. Motorsports Images & Archives Photo

available. When Allison wasn't tearing up a superspeedway, he was probably on some short track, revving up his engine and bursting through the corners with a bevy of competitors on his back bumper.

He won 84 NASCAR Winston Cup races, a list capped when he edged his son, Davey, in the 1988 Daytona 500. Soon after, he was injured in an accident and forced to retire.

Buddy Baker, the son of Buck Baker, stood out in size alone. Towering six foot five and weighing more than 200 pounds, he was a giant among the drivers and knew only one approach to driving. "Pell-mell pedal pushing," one writer in 1982 described Baker's method. "Running on the ragged edge of control was a spur of the moment sprint for him; it's been his style. He has driven like there's a burr under his bottom."

In 1970, he became the first driver to cross the 200-mph barrier on a closed circuit by clocking 200.447 mph at Talladega Superspeedway. Speed did not translate into trophies. Baker's cars often broke down under his lead-footed efforts. He still won 19 races, including the 1983 Firecracker 400.

Ned Jarrett is better known these days in his role as a television commentator. In the 1960s, the North Carolinian was a terror on the track. In 1965, for example, Jarrett finished in the top five in 42 of 54 races. He eventually won 50 races from 1953 through 1966 and two championships. His son, Dale, won the 1999 title, making the Jarretts one of only two father-son combinations to take home racing's top prize. Lee and Richard Petty are the others on this elite list.

Fred Lorenzen ran in seven NASCAR Winston Cup races in 1956. Five years later, the Illinois native began plastering his name all over the record book for races of 250 miles or longer. He eventually won 26 races, 23 of them in races of 250 miles or longer, including the 1965 Daytona 500. He won 12 superspeedway races, a record at the time. He was Ford's "Golden Boy" when, on April 24, 1967, he shocked the racing world by retiring at 32. He would return briefly before leaving the sport for good in 1972.

"That was a mistake retiring when I did," said Lorenzen. "If I had to do it over, I would have raced longer."

He also would have raced more often. Lorenzen never ran the full schedule. In 1963, for example, he entered 29 of 55 races and finished third in the point standings. He also became the first driver to win more than $100,000 in a season. In 1964, he ran only 16 races and won eight. His final win came at Daytona International Speedway in the second 100-mile qualifying race in 1967. He went the distance without a pit stop while everyone else paused for refueling. Lorenzen was a master at drafting and getting better gas mileage than anybody. The following year, NASCAR bumped up the races to 125 miles.

David Pearson, the "Silver Fox," was Petty's chief rival from 1960 through 1986. He holds 20 different records, including most consecutive top-five finishes (18 in 1968) and best winning percentage (61 percent in 1973). In 1988, he was labeled "perhaps the best race-for-race driver of all time."

Quick work by the Wood Brothers helped David Pearson set a record by leading 491 of 492 laps here at North Carolina Speedway in 1973. Motorsports Images & Archives Photo

Petty went further and said he was the "best all-around driver NASCAR has" after Pearson posted victories in 1970 on short tracks, road courses and superspeedways.

The South Carolina legend won three championships from 1960 through 1986, finishing first or second 194 times in 574 races.

Cale Yarborough began his career in 1957, but didn't get rolling until the mid-1960s. He eventually posted 83 wins and is the only driver to win three championships in a row. Speed was his calling card: 15 times in his career, Yarborough topped 200 mph in qualifying, the most of any driver.

Other famed drivers from these years include Donnie Allison, Benny Parsons and LeeRoy Yarbrough.

Through it all, as drivers and manufacturers came and went, there was one constant. Bill France remained at the helm. That finally changed, too. One year short of NASCAR's silver anniversary, he retired, turning control of the sanctioning body to his two sons, Bill and Jim.

His departure in 1972 was a fitting climax for an era that began with the opening of the Daytona International Speedway and ended when the last of the beach racers finally went home for good.

chapter eleven

1972-81

The Modern Era brought with it new challenges, ranging from an energy crisis to rising expenses that reduced entries, a muddled point system and strained resources. Interest in stock-car racing, however, zoomed. By the middle of the 1970s, NASCAR took the lead in worldwide motorsports attendance, a position it has not lost since.

The sport also picked up another distinction, something the grimy, oil-stained mechanics who fiddled over their engines and tried to keep them running through a complete race, would never have imagined.

"When we built the track," Bill France said in 1978, "we didn't have the ocean any longer, but we had a new glamour."

It was a powerful magnet. Paul Newman, the famous actor, came to Daytona Beach to race in what became the Rolex 24 at Daytona. He would be joined at various times by such popular figures as actors James Garner, Tim Allen, Craig T. Nelson, Bobby Carradine, Jason Priestley, and country-western singer Marty Robbins. Robbins actually got into the 1973 Daytona 500, but wrecked on the 66th lap. From that point on, he was kiddingly nicknamed "NASCAR's official wall tester."

Georgia Governor Jimmy Carter told the *Washington Star* prior to the 1976 presidential election, "Stock car racing is my favorite sport." The newspaper light-heartedly warned readers they'd have to expect some changes in the inaugural parade if Carter beat incumbent President Gerald Ford, including a lead car with the name of

Reticent around reporters, David Pearson let his driving
do his talking for him. The South Carolina native was
considered the greatest driver of his era. Motorsports Images
& Archives Photo

a sponsor painted on its side. After the election, Carter's brother Billy showed up at the 1977 race.

Daytona was becoming the place to be in February for more than race fans.

Television helped generate that kind of attention. In 1974, ABC televised the last two hours of the Daytona 500. After watching ratings for races outpace competing sporting events, other networks began to bring their cameras to various tracks. In 1979, the Daytona 500 was telecast live in its entirety for the first time.

The early years of television had not polished the drivers. They were still the same roughnecks who battled on and off the track, waged feuds, threw punches and helped produce the aura of spontaneity and excitement surrounding the sport.

Clifton "Coo Coo" Marlin had to talk his way out of jail simply to compete in the 1972 Firecracker 400 after he, his wife, Eula Faye and fellow drivers Elmo Langley and Dub Simpson got too near a brawl at a Daytona Beach nightspot. One of the two men fighting nearby accidentally struck Marlin's wife. The Tennessean promptly jumped into the battle along with his colleagues.

"We were ahead when the police finally came by," Marlin reported proudly.

That was nothing compared to various race-related squabbles involving Cale Yarborough against the Allison brothers, then Richard Petty vs. Bobby Allison and David Pearson.

In 1979, in the Daytona 500, Yarborough and Donnie Allison spun each other out on the last lap. Allison had made up one lap in the race and Yarborough three before the two collided when Allison blocked Yarborough's attempt to slingshot him. After the race, won by Petty, Yarborough took a swing at Bobby Allison, who had stopped to check on the condition of his brother.

"I hit Bobby because he just smarted off," Yarborough explained.

The scrap about a mile from the finish line was captured by television cameras. "Millions of people who had never watched an auto race before had just seen NASCAR's finest duke it out," historian Neely wrote.

Donnie Allison was placed on probation by NASCAR for taking up too much of the track.

Bobby Allison and Richard Petty took turns bumping each other into the walls in the mid-1970s. They both denied feuding until it was too obvious to paper over. NASCAR officials finally forced them to shake hands.

Petty and David Pearson also locked horns, culminating in the 1976 Daytona 500. Problems had started in the 1974 Firecracker 400. Pretend-

Television discovered the Daytona 500 in the 1960s, bringing such commentators as former Grand Prix racers Jackie Stewart (left) and Sterling Moss to add glamour to "The Great American Race." In 1979, CBS began to broadcast the race from green flag to Victory Lane. Motorsports Images & Archives Photo

David Pearson, his car battered after a collision with Richard Petty (rear) on the last lap of the 1976 Daytona 500, slowly limps across the start/finish line to record his lone win in "The Great American Race." **Motorsports Images & Archives Photo**

ing his car was having engine problems, Pearson slowed on the final lap and let Petty pass. Then, the "Silver Fox" slyly sped up and used Petty's patented slingshot move to pass "The King" to record his third straight win in the event.

Petty was furious, accusing Pearson of making a dangerous move. "What he did was risky and unnecessary," he stormed.

"I didn't think it was a risky move," Pearson responded. "I pulled to the inside of the track on the straightaway, and I don't think I endangered him."

Only the royal pride was hurt.

The friction increased in 1975 in the Daytona 500 when, during the race, Petty waved to Benny

Parsons and invited the former taxi driver from Detroit to follow him. The two drafted together and quickly erased Pearson's comfortable lead. Pearson saw them coming, ended up losing control and swiped Cale Yarborough's slower car.

Parsons, now a popular television commentator, got the trophy. Pearson got the blues. "I got spun out, but I'd rather not talk about it," the normally reticent South Carolinian said. "People who were watching know who did it."

Those two races set the stage for the 1976 Daytona 500, one of the most controversial final laps in racing lore and "the most dramatic finish in NASCAR history," according to Bob Hoffman of the *Southern Motorsports Journal*.

Pearson and Petty headed into the last lap virtually side by side. Pearson had never won the prestigious event and was desperate for a visit to Victory Lane. Petty was equally desperate to keep his rival winless.

Diving low on the backstretch, Pearson inched ahead. Petty caught him on Turn 3. "At the point where the banked turn begins to flatten out, Petty's Dodge started to drift toward the right, toward the outside wall and back toward the racing groove," author Tucker reported. "Petty's right rear fender clipped the left front of Pearson's Mercury."

The son of one long-time NASCAR competitor and the nephew of another, Davey Allison was a rising star when he was killed in a helicopter crash at Talladega in 1993. Motorsports Images & Archives Photo

Pearson was aware exactly what was going to happen next, Tucker continued. "Pearson, rim-riding in the higher, faster, racing lane, was guarding his ground and did not ease off the throttle to allow Petty enough room to come back into the racing groove. Pearson knew it probably meant both cars would wreck. To hold his car wide open at that moment must have taken tremendous courage."

The Dodge and Mercury smashed together. After bumping the wall, Pearson's car headed south, sliding toward the entrance to pit row. A slower car, driven by Joe Frasson, clipped him there, leaving him seemingly stranded perhaps three-quarters of a mile from the checkered flag. Ahead of him, Petty spun wildly off the wall and ended up on the infield grass, perhaps 35 feet short of the finish line.

Somehow, while careening around the track, "Pearson had the presence of mind to push down his clutch and keep his car's engine running," Tucker recorded. Petty, meanwhile, was helpless. His engine had stalled. His crew ran to assist him.

Pearson shouted into his radio, "Where's Petty? Where's Petty? Did he get across the finish line?"

"No," a crewmember called back.

With Pearson stepping on the gas, his battered car began to spit out grass and dirt, inching slowly back to the race. Pearson stayed on the bottom of the track and limped under the checkered flag at 20 mph for his lone Daytona 500 victory. Behind him, Petty's crew desperately tried to push the heavy Dodge the last few feet. Petty still ended up second, although he was fined later for receiving outside assistance.

Asked what he was thinking when the crash occurred, Petty answered dryly, "I wasn't exactly hollering 'Hooray for me.'"

Later, Petty apologized to Pearson for making contact, author Neely recorded. "That's all right," Pearson told him. "You didn't mean to do it."

Roughhousing was not the only tradition drivers in the 1970s kept alive. Cheating was commonplace. In 1973, Charlie Glotzbach was forced to re-qualify at Charlotte after officials found an illegal car-

Cale Yarborough is the only driver to win three consecutive NASCAR Winston Cup championships, but was nearing retirement in 1987. Motorsports Images & Archives Photo

buretor plate that could be removed by tugging on a cable in the cockpit. Bobby Allison promptly accused everyone else in the race of cheating and demanded inspections of the top two cars, including Petty's famous No. 43. When NASCAR declined to change the results, despite evidence of altered engines, Allison threatened to file suit.

The drumbeat of publicity continued for weeks, until Bill France met with Allison. France may have retired, but he still was chairman of the board. Allison backed down, and everyone went back to racing.

In 1976, most of the top qualifiers for the Daytona 500 were disqualified after NASCAR technicians found "fuel pressure assists." (Janet Guthrie later that year drove one of the disqualified cars—after it passed inspection—and finished

15th in a race.) Dave Marcis, who retired in 2002, lost his spot because of a "moveable air-deflector device placed in front of the radiator."

On A.J. Foyt's car, officials found a bottle of nitrous oxide, commonly called "laughing gas." Poured into the engine, it provided a quick burst of about 50 horsepower, something that was not funny to fellow competitors.

Legendary mechanic Smokey Yunick shrugged when told about it. "I was using nitrous oxide back in the 1940s and 1950s," he said. "It wasn't spelled out in the rule book, and therefore it wasn't illegal." By this time, use of it certainly was.

Driver Ed Negre, whose sponsor was a company that distributed nitrous oxide, said the only reason the drivers got caught in 1976 was because their competitors drove deliberately slower to make the disparity in qualifying times look suspicious. "It was all a plan," he claimed. "I didn't run because my bottle was hooked up, and I didn't want NASCAR to find it." Nigre was disqualified the day before the race when officials found the bottle hooked up in his Dodge.

Everyone was looking for an edge. "In Grand National racing," said Darrell Waltrip, an outspoken driver who retired at the end of the 2000 sea-

Richard Petty (top) spins wildly after colliding with David Pearson. Petty would eventually settle in the infield grass, unable to move as Pearson limped his damaged car across the finish line in one of the most dramatic Daytona 500 finishes.

Motorsports Images & Archives Photo

son to become a television commentator, "there are a lot of things you have to do to keep up with the competition. It's common knowledge that cheating in one form or another is part of it. If you don't cheat, you look like an idiot. If you do it and don't get caught, you look like a hero."

Despite the occasional rough spots on the track, events outside the sport had the biggest impact on the entire racing world. The energy crisis in 1973 threatened to curtail the entire 1974 season. Members of the Organization of Petroleum Exporting Countries (OPEC) had decided to cut oil supplies to the United States after the success Israel enjoyed in the October 1973 war against its surrounding Arab neighbors. The Arab leaders of the oil cartel blamed the United States for supporting Israel.

As lines grew at gas stations and supplies dried up, the government began to look for ways to cut usage. Racing, which is totally dependent on gasoline, was a prime target.

A government study of consumption found that racing was seventh on the list of top users, consuming 93.6 million gallons of fuel a year. Bill France Jr. came up with another interesting fact: "It takes less fuel to run a 500-mile auto race than it does to fly the Washington Redskins to a pro football game on the West Coast. And that's all the cars involved."

Racing was not halted, despite some demands for that remedy, but the federal government requested that all industries cut gasoline use by 20 to 25 percent.

NASCAR complied by reducing races during the first half of the 1974 season by 10 percent. That included the Daytona 500, which became 50 miles shorter. Practice time was cut from eight to five hours, and teams were restricted to 30 gallons of gasoline during practice. The restrictions actually sliced consumption by more than 30 percent. Having beat the government cutback request, NASCAR began to run full races later in the year, starting with the 1974 Firecracker 400.

While that problem was easy to resolve, working out a viable point system was much more difficult. Various approaches were tried, including giving points for each lap or based on money won. The system at one point was changed five times in six years. The current method awards 175 points to the winner with every entrant receiving points down to 34 for the last-place competitor. In addition, anyone who leads a single lap gets a five-point bonus. Another five points is given to the driver who leads the most laps. The system has kept championship races tight in most years, boosting interest among fans and drivers.

While tinkering went on with the points, other concerns revved up. The number of entrants started to shrink as costs rose. New rules designed to increase safety and even up competition began to crimp pocketbooks. In 1973, only one driver, an independent named Frank Warren, made every race. Richard Petty was the lone driver who made any effort to win the championship.

OPPOSITE: Dale Earnhardt is the only driver to grab the Raybestos Rookie of the Year Award in the NASCAR Winston Cup Series one year, then win the championship the following season.
Motorsports Images & Archives Photo

To increase participation, NASCAR began openly paying appearance fees to the top teams representing each of the four manufacturers. More was paid to the top teams that competed in races from 400 to 600 miles long and lesser amounts for races from 250 to 300 miles. The amounts were paltry by modern standards—$2,500 for a long race—but often made the difference. Teams needed every cent.

In 1959, Cotton Owens could tell the *Daytona Beach Morning Journal* that he was able to clock in at 153.19 mph in Daytona time trials with a car built by hand from parts of "two 1958 Pontiacs which had been wrecked in a junkyard" two weeks previously. Owens and mechanic Louis Clements "used one half of one and half of the other to build the car I raced today for the first time at racing speed."

Less than 20 years later, Owens's method of producing a race car seemed absurd. Crew chiefs could no longer go to junkyards and part stores to find replacement equipment. Engines had to be torn down after every event and key components replaced. Costs were beginning to skyrocket.

Moreover, factory support had vanished. The constant withdrawal and re-entry of Chrysler, Ford and Chevrolet had eroded the fiscal base of teams. By 1971, virtually all the manufacturers had stopped paying drivers to drive their products.

"We reached a point where we had everything to lose and nothing to gain," a Chrysler spokesman said. He cited constant rule changes that continually frustrated attempts to insert new cars into the races.

NASCAR, however, was not unhappy. "The trouble has been that factories tried to control the sport," explained Lin Kuchler, then-NASCAR vice president. "The difficulty came on our end when we didn't feel a car conformed to our specifications. It became a question of us backing down or sticking to our guns and making them comply."

The loss of support from Ford, Dodge, General Motors and Chrysler left only corporations with the deep pockets available to fund race cars. Richard Petty, the leader of the top NASCAR series, signed up STP, which remained his team's primary sponsor until 2000. Other drivers were not so lucky and were forced to procure new sponsors virtually on an annual basis.

The arrival of R.J. Reynolds Tobacco in 1972 helped mitigate some of the expenses. The company created a postseason fund, now more than $3 million, to reward the top drivers in the standings and boosted purses. The company also changed the face of NASCAR by insisting all races be at least 250 miles long.

That requirement eliminated many of the smaller tracks, helping pare back the schedule. The 1972 season consisted of 31 races in what was known as the NASCAR Winston Cup Grand National Series. The smaller tracks were united in a division called Grand National East. A similar set up was arranged across the country under the name Grand National West (now West Series).

While the support from a tobacco company was extremely helpful, it carried a stigma. Cigarette manufacturers were banned from radio and television commercials in 1971 in a growing drive

STARS SHINE ON DAYTONA

The growing significance in the Daytona 500 in American culture is reflected in the array of celebrities who choose to spend part of February in Daytona Beach.

Actor John Travolta gave a stirring command to start engines as the Grand Marshal for the 45th running of "The Great American Race" in 2003 while Grammy Award-winning artist Mariah Carey, the biggest-selling female pop artist of all time, sang the national anthem and waved the green flag to get the historic race underway.

Also in attendance at "The World Center of Racing" for the Daytona 500 were tennis ace Serena Williams, skateboarding icon Tony Hawk, *American Idol* judge Randy Jackson, action movie actor Vin Diesel, boxer Evander Holyfield and Travolta's wife and actress Kelly Preston.

Two-time Emmy-nominated comic actor Wayne Brady performed at the exclusive Grand Marshal's dinner.

They are all following in well-worn footprints. Entertainers like James Garner, Lily Tomlin, Roy Rogers, Ben Gazarra and Paul Newman have all been there during Speedweeks. Singer Marty Robbins drove in the Daytona 500.

Former President George H.W. Bush has attended three different races at the world-famous Speedway. As director of the CIA, he served as Grand Marshal of the 1978 Daytona 500; as Vice President, he was Honorary Starter of the 1983 Daytona 500; and as President, he served as Grand Marshal of the 1992 Pepsi 400.

Supreme Court Justice Clarence Thomas presided as Grand Marshal over the 1999 Daytona 500.

---

to cut consumption. To prevent loss of support from Reynolds, NASCAR prohibited all other tobacco companies as sponsors and decreed that decals advertising tobacco products could not be larger than four inches by eight inches. In 2001, tobacco companies were ordered to reduce sponsorship to a single sports outlet. R.J. Reynolds chose NASCAR. Only in 2003, when restrictions made promoting its products difficult and rising lawsuits cut into profits did the tobacco company decide to pull out of its new five-year contract with NASCAR midway through its run.

Nextel, a telecommunications company, beat out several competitors to sign a 10-year deal with NASCAR that began in 2004.

RJR remained with NASCAR for 33 years, building its own business as racing caught on as a national pastime. A new generation of fans, weaned on television, had become enamored with the sport. The many great races of the decade caught their fancy; the aura that now surrounded racing kept them intrigued. As in every era, something unusual invariably happened on the track, especially at Daytona where everyone desperately wanted to win.

In the 1977 Firecracker 400, three women competed in the same race for the first time since 1949. Janet Guthrie, Christine Beckers and Lella Lombardi all failed to complete the event, which was won by Richard Petty.

In the 1978 Daytona 500, Petty blew a tire and took out Waltrip and Pearson at the same time. A.J. Foyt was eliminated in another mishap started by Benny Parsons's blown tire. Bobby Allison skirted

Richard Petty made this car world famous. His father, Lee, drove the No. 42. His son, Kyle, drove the No. 44; and grandson Adam took No. 45. Kyle moved to the No. 45 after Adam was killed in a mishap during practice. Motorsports Images & Archives Photo

all the confusion to win, breaking a 67-race losing streak.

In the 1978 Firecracker 400, Pearson got around Baxter Price, then used the slower car to block an onrushing Cale Yarborough. "I wish I could have disappeared," Price said.

In 1981, Richard Petty took his seventh and final Daytona 500 by driving the last 162.5 miles on the same set of tires. With the win, Petty also recorded the first victory by a Buick since 1955. Rookie Geoffrey Bodine spiced up the proceedings by sliding through Turn 4 and into the infield. His Pontiac scaled a dirt embankment and mashed a car belonging to a local television station.

By then, the whole image of NASCAR had begun to change. While the general public still considered the drivers uneducated yokels fresh from the mountains, the media began to notice a difference. The patina of breeding only went so far. When Junior Johnson was asked to wear a tie before going into a posh New York nightclub prior to the annual NASCAR Winston Cup banquet in New York, he stalked out and ate a hotdog on a street corner.

At the end of the 1977 season, however, nine of the top drivers went to a conference in New York. They must have made a positive impression on the sports journalists who interviewed them. One of the writers told author Neely, "This is the greatest transition the sport has ever gone through—having drivers with the ability to speak."

The most vocal was Waltrip, who picked up the nickname "Jaws" from Cale Yarborough. The Kentucky native would eventually win 84 races in his career along with three NASCAR Winston Cup championships. Voted driver of the decade in the 1980s, Waltrip began his career racing against drivers like Richard Petty, Coo Coo Marlin and Bobby Allison, and ended it racing their children, grandchildren or drivers in cars owned by his former competitors.

"I didn't have the greatest equipment in the beginning to compete with them," Waltrip said. "So, I found another way." He almost invented psychological warfare on the track by openly challenging the top drivers. That routine started in the 1960s when Nashville promoter Bill Donoho paid him a little extra to spice things up with comments made on live radio and television shows.

"I'd stir the pot, trying to get people to fill the grandstands," Waltrip said. "That meant extra money for me."

He carried that same technique into NASCAR. Then he backed it up with results. "I'm an impact player," Waltrip said. "I didn't come into this sport just to hang out."

He wasn't the only one with plans to make a splash. A series of younger drivers began to find spots in the starting grid during this decade. They would be the competitors who carried NASCAR to greater heights, moving stock-car racing onto the same level as professional baseball, basketball and football.

Dale Earnhardt showed up in 1975 and got a full-time ride in 1979. The son of a Late-Model Sportsman champ, Earnhardt got his start on short tracks around his native North Carolina. Named Raybestos Rookie of the Year in 1979, he was the first to win the championship the following year.

Tough and blessed with a "go-for-broke attitude" that propelled him on a mad dash for Victory Lane, he became known as "The Man in Black" or "The Intimidator." He was also smart, trademarking his signature No. 3 to become a multimillionaire. Earnhardt, who died in 2001, backed up his business acumen with success on the track, winning a record-tying seven championships and 76 victories in 675 starts.

He built his reputation in Daytona where he won 34 races, including 10 straight Gatorade 125s.

His lone Daytona 500 victory in 1998 took him 20 years to achieve and may have been the most emotional win in the long history of racing's paramount event.

Terry Labonte also started in 1979 and became the first man to capture NASCAR Winston Cup championships 12 years apart. The Texan showed off some of his ability in his initial race by finishing fourth at Darlington Raceway in 1978. The "iron man" of racing, nicknamed "Iceman," Labonte held the record of 655 consecutive starts, which was broken in 2002 by Ricky Rudd, and is one of only seven drivers with at least 700 starts.

Rudd began his career in 1975 and, in 2001, joined Labonte on that list with more than 700 starts. Raybestos Rookie of the Year in 1977, the Virginian won races in 16 consecutive years, tying the modern era record.

Rusty Wallace got his first start in 1980. One of three racing brothers, the St. Louis native finished second to Earnhardt in his debut race, but didn't get a full-time ride until 1984. He won Raybestos Rookie of the Year honors that season and has gone on to match Rudd with at least one win in 16 consecutive seasons.

With drivers like that on the track, Daytona had no trouble retaining its place as the kingpin of racing.

The success of Darrell Waltrip, who was born in Kentucky, helped signal the end of Carolina dominance in the NASCAR Winston Cup Series. Waltrip won three championships and was the leading driver of the 1980s.
Motorsports Images & Archives Photo

Dale Earnhardt Jr. (No. 8) and Tony Stewart (No. 20) are two of the most popular drivers in the NASCAR NEXTEL Cup Series. Both earn millions of dollars a year based on their skills behind the wheel and through souvenir sales. **Motorsports Images & Archives Photo**

chapter twelve

1982-2003

When 1982 dawned, the sun shone brightly on Daytona Beach. The year introduced a massive change in the season schedule and launched a 20-year run to international recognition. During the next two-plus decades, NASCAR Winston Cup drivers achieved status on par with any athletes in any sport. Drivers like Dale Earnhardt Jr. and Jeff Gordon are now pocketing an estimated $30 to $60 million a year in prize money, endorsements and sales of souvenirs. Gordon, who joined the NASCAR Winston Cup Series full time in 1993, has led a stampede from open-wheel racing into stock cars, shifting the balance away from Indy Cars in national prestige. Tony Stewart, Ryan Newman, Jason Leffler, John Andretti, Casey Mears, Christian Fittipaldi and Robby Gordon have followed in his wide tire tracks. New facilities now present NASCAR races in parts of the country unseen since the beach events, while virtually every stock car and truck race in NASCAR's major series is broadcast in its entirety on a national basis.

Televised coverage of the Daytona 500 provided a main impetus. Drivers were suddenly in the media spotlight. With no other major motorsports events held anywhere in the world during February, Daytona garnered complete attention.

It also helped that NASCAR changed the NEXTEL Cup schedule. While the Daytona 500 was the most important race in any year, it was not the one that kicked off

OPPOSITE: **Ryan Newman (No. 12) begins to flip on lap 57 of the 2003 Daytona 500.**
Motorsports Images & Archives Photo

Rival teams lined up in 1998 to congratulate Dale Earnhardt (No. 3) after his long-anticipated victory in the Daytona 500. Motorsports Images & Archives Photo

the season. That had been true even before the building of Daytona International Speedway, except for a couple of years when the series began.

The race on the old Beach-Road Course had been second on the schedule in 1949, NASCAR's first full season. No one seemed to think it should be the lead-off event. It was simply the most important. A year later, without apparent comment, the season opened in Daytona for a 200-mile race. In those days, that was a lengthy race. Only the Southern 500 at Darlington race was longer. In 1951, Daytona had the honors again, this time for a 160-mile race.

Then, it was moved from the start of the season, again without comment. In these early years, NASCAR was only trying to survive and create some sort of following, principally among race-loving constituents in the South. Races were scheduled wherever tracks could be found. The beach, after all, was going to be there regardless of when the race was held. Since it was in Daytona, with its long history, any event there would always have special significance.

So, in 1952, the racers started their season at Palm Beach Speedway in West Palm Beach, Florida. They stayed there for the next three years, then returned again in 1956. Originally a half-mile dirt track, it was paved in 1955 but not used after the race the following year.

With the move to West Palm Beach, the Daytona race on the Beach-Road Course was relegated to the second race of the year, held on the second or third Sunday in February. That seemed to set a precedent. For years, even when the location of the season opener shifted, as it did several times, the Daytona 500 did not initiate the racing season.

The situation got almost bizarre some years. The Grand National Division kicked off its 1957 season with a race in November 1956 at Willow Springs International Raceway in Lancaster, California. Two other races were held in 1956 before the new year began with the annual race on the beach course, placing it fourth on the schedule. In both 1958 and 1959, the season opened with events at Champion Speedway in Fayetteville, N.C. Daytona was second on the schedule in 1958. That was unchanged in 1959, despite construction of the new speedway.

In essence, the Daytona 500 had become the first race of the year, but not the first in the new season.

In 1960 and 1961, Charlotte (N.C.) Fairgrounds held the honors as Daytona was placed third. By then, the Daytona race had stabilized at

500 miles (the beach race was 160 miles), even if the schedule was still shifting like sand in the tide.

In 1962, the season debuted at Concord (North Carolina) Speedway and remained in the East until 1964. Then, without explanation, the entire series shifted to California to begin the 1965 season. That move only lasted a year, before everyone motored back across the continent to kick off the 1966 season at Augusta, Georgia.

After four years in Georgia, the California rush was on again. From 1970 until 1981, everyone traipsed across the country to find the gold in Victory Lane at Riverside (California) International Raceway. The races took place in January with

Alan Kulwicki was the last independent driver to win the NASCAR Winston Cup Series title. He edged Bill Elliott by 10 points in 1992, the closest championship race in series history.
Motorsports Images & Archives Photo

Speedweeks showing up at its regular February berth.

Finally, February 14, 1982, Daytona Beach became the home of the first race of the season. For the first time in 30 years, the entire focus of the racing world was on the community where racing began.

In traditional Daytona fashion, the 1982 race was a bit unusual. Prior to the race, Bobby Allison's crew was ordered to make an adjustment to the placement of the rear bumper on the No. 88 Buick. Ten laps into the event, Cale Yarborough bumped into Allison coming off Turn 4. The 20-pound bumper went flying, causing a five-car pileup.

Yarborough had to stop for repairs. Allison's car became looser, but he was able to overpower the field to win by 22.87 seconds.

After the race, Yarborough's crew chief Tim Brewer suggested to reporters that the bumper had been designed to fall off.

"I make a lot of excuses when I don't win," Allison replied, "so I don't pay any attention to anyone else's excuses."

The next year, Yarborough set an unofficial qualifying record by topping 200.503 mph. He promptly crashed on his second qualifying lap and ended up starting in a back-up car in eighth place. Undaunted, he finally slingshotted Buddy Baker on the last lap to win by about four car lengths.

In 1987, Bill Elliott would top Yarborough's record run by posting 210.253 mph. He became the fastest driver in Daytona Beach since Major Segrave and Malcolm Campbell rode their rocket ships across the hard beach sand more than 50 years earlier.

By then, the Daytona 500 was established as the first race, and the most important one, of the season. Speedweeks evolved into 16 days of racing, starting with the around-the-clock Rolex 24 marathon and ending with the climactic Daytona 500.

The shift in scheduling generated a spotlight that focused totally on Daytona Beach for two full weeks. Other major series, like the Indy Racing League and CART, hold their first races later in the year, leaving Daytona Beach alone to bask in the media glare.

The added attention increased the importance of the race and brought more celebrities into the mix. President Ronald Reagan became the first chief executive to serve as honorary grand marshal when he came to the Firecracker 400 in 1984.

Unlike other sports, drivers are accessible to fans. Jeff Gordon signs autographs prior to the 2003 Daytona 500. As interest in racing has grown, NASCAR has been forced to limit contact. Motorsports Images & Archives Photo

The pre-race lineup is a confusing mixture of crews, fans, media and drivers, all waiting for the familiar call: "Gentlemen, start your engines." Motorsports Images & Archives Photo

In 1990, two cars ran the race with cameras, filming for what would become the *Days of Thunder* movie featuring Tom Cruise and Nicole Kidman. Many other actors and actresses have been spotted attending the Daytona 500 and the surrounding festivities.

By 1993, 11 years after the Daytona 500 had taken the limelight for itself, Richard Petty was being asked by Ted Koppel on ABC's *Nightline* why auto racing had become this country's most highly attended sport.

Petty was not sure what to say. He remains a living link to the days when cars raced on beaches and then onto dinky half-mile dirt tracks in front of a few thousand people. He has seen the sport grow so dramatically that his total career earnings of $7.75 million was topped by Jeff Gordon in a single year. Finally, he told Koppel that racing was a sport of "competition, emotion and people."

All of that was encapsulated in a single race.

Because of the significance of the Daytona 500, drivers felt added pressure to win. They all knew it.

"This is the race," said Jeff Gordon after his win in 1997. "This is the big one, the one we really wanted."

A year later, after Dale Earnhardt finally earned his first Daytona 500 victory, the seven-time champion, who notched 76 career wins, told reporters, "Winning the Daytona 500 is what it's all about. This is what everyone works for."

Three-time Daytona 500 winner Dale Jarrett said, "When you win here, you know you've beaten the best at their best."

This is the Harley J. Earl Trophy given to the winner of the Daytona 500. The car on top is not the Bluebird driven to world-speed records, but the Firebird, a futuristic 1950s car imagined by the legendary General Motors designer. Motorsports Images & Archives Photo

Added Terry Labonte, who has won two championships but never visited Victory Lane in Daytona, "If you can only win one race, this is it."

As a result, the recent Daytona 500s have often featured some of the most riveting contents and unusual mishaps in NASCAR Winston Cup history. Besides Earnhardt's emotional win in 1998, two of the most incredible events took place in 1988 and in 2001.

In 1988, Bobby Allison a holdover from the old days, raced against his son, Davey, representing the new breed of racers. Davey had grown up watching his father—just as Dale Jarrett, Dale Earnhardt, Kyle Petty and Sterling Marlin, among others, watched their fathers compete—and followed him into racing. No other sport features so many sons chasing after their fathers' exploits. In

this race, more history was made when Bobby and Davey became the first father and son to finish 1-2 in "The Great American Race."

For the last 10 laps, the two raced nose to tail. Davey continually got under his father's rear spoiler, but simply couldn't find the power to get around his dad's Buick. This was the first race run at Daytona with a restrictor plate. It slowed the times, but not the action. "It was a tight race with a lot of mental pressure," Bobby said. "If you made a mistake, you'd go back to 15th or 20th place. It was an on-the-edge-of-the-seat race."

The win capped Bobby Allison's career. An on-track accident four months later forced him to retire. Davey, who later won the 1992 Daytona 500, was killed in a 1993 helicopter crash.

Another legendary driver also neared the end of his career in the 1988 race. Richard Petty was tapped by Phil Barkdoll and lost control of his car on Turn 4 late in the race. His Pontiac was bumped into the wall, spun on its nose, barrel-rolled 12 times and took out 20 feet of grandstand fence. After finally landing on its four tires, Petty was run into by another racing legend, A.J. Foyt.

"When he came down," Foyt said, "I hit his left side with my right side."

Petty wasn't done yet. His crippled car was then smacked by Brett Bodine, tearing off the front end and spinning it like a top. "The end of the career of Richard Petty," announcer Chris Economaki speculated on national television. Unbelievably, Petty walked away unscathed, a testament to the stamina of the drivers and to their safety equipment.

In 2001, the rules had changed. A new aerodynamic package, based on one that made the previous fall race at Talladega Superspeedway a classic, was tried at Daytona for the first time.

As a result, the 43rd edition of "The Great American race" was one for the record books. The first surprise came before the green flag waved. Veteran Bill Elliott grabbed the Bud Pole in a Dodge, which was returning to NASCAR Winston Cup for the first time since 1985. Stacy Compton, also in a Dodge, sat beside him.

Fourteen drivers swapped the lead 49 times, not counting the multiple lead changes within laps. A driver could be in the lead one minute and shuffled back to 10th the next. Elliott lost the lead on the first lap and was far back in the pack within a few more laps. Rusty Wallace cut a tire, lost a lap, then gained it back.

"It was great racing," said Jeff Gordon, who has won the Daytona 500 twice.

Late in the race, Dale Earnhardt Jr. and his late father battled with Dale Jr.'s teammate, Michael Waltrip, right behind. Waltrip, who hadn't won in a record 462 NASCAR Winston Cup starts, had been a surprise addition to the Earnhardt team over the winter.

On lap 183, Waltrip managed to get around Marlin and then Earnhardt. Dale Jr. locked onto his rear spoiler. Earnhardt tucked into third as the three cars streaked in tandem around the track.

In the television booth, Darrell Waltrip watched his younger brother maintain the lead. Tears filled his eyes. "My baby brother's leading it," he exclaimed with six laps to go. His emotion reminded onlookers of when Ned Jarrett cheered on his son's first Daytona 500 victory back in 1993.

As the laps slowly ran out, Michael Waltrip was stunned. "I couldn't believe it was going to play out," he said. "I finally believed I was going to win with five laps to go."

Trailed by his teammate, Waltrip crossed the finish line .124 seconds ahead of Earnhardt Jr. He joined Darrell as the only brothers to win the Daytona 500. Moreover, no one had come from as far back as 19th place to win since Bobby Allison started 33rd in 1978 en route to the checkered flag.

He was also the sixth driver to win his first career race at the Daytona 500 in the memorable history of "The Great American Race." Sterling Marlin (1994) was the last to accomplish that feat before Waltrip. Derrike Cope (1990), Pete Hamilton (1970), Mario Andretti (1967) and Tiny Lund (1963) were the others.

Dale Earnhardt, the man who for millions of race fans embodied the sport, never saw the end. Caught up in a final-lap accident, he died after his famed No. 3 Goodwrench Chevrolet smacked the wall head on.

Kevin Harvick was then given the ride in the car, going on to finish in the top 10 in the 2001 standings and winning the Rookie of the Year award.

In between those two classics, there have been other memorable Daytona 500s:

• In 1985, Bill Elliott won the Daytona 500 en route to winning the $1 million bonus for three victories in the same year at Daytona, Talladega, Darlington and Charlotte. "Awesome Bill" would go on to become one of NASCAR's most popular drivers ever. He would never forget this race, although the Georgian won at Daytona again in 1987. "If I never win again," he said in 1985, "this will be very special to me."

• In 1989, an emotional Darrell Waltrip ran out of gas crossing the finish line in first place. "I won the Daytona 500?" he cried in Victory Lane. "Oh, thank God. I'm not dreaming, am I? This is Daytona, isn't it?"

• In 1990, in perhaps the biggest upset in Daytona 500 history, Derrike Cope passed Dale Earnhardt one mile from the finish line to win the first race of his career. Earnhardt had hit a piece of metal, puncturing his right tire. "I was hoping to get to the start-finish line, but didn't make it," he said glumly "They didn't outrun us; they lucked into it."

• In 1992, Richard Petty ended his remarkable career by serving as grand marshal and also driving. This time, Davey Allison won, joining his father, Bobby, and Lee and Richard Petty as the only fathers and sons to win at Daytona.

• Earnhardt would earn his lone Daytona 500 victory in 1998. After he crossed the finish line, members of every team lined up to congratulate the fierce competitor who had taken their sport to the highest level.

• Because the Pepsi 400 is also held at Daytona International Speedway, it also has developed an aura of its own.

No "Summer Classic" probably created more emotion than the 1984 race. The 16th race of the season, the Pepsi 400 drew President Reagan and more than 80,000 spectators hoping to see Richard Petty record his 200th career victory.

Petty and Cale Yarborough battled for the lead late in the race. On lap 157, Doug Heveron nearly flipped, bringing out a caution. Whoever got back to the start-finish line first would win, since there would be no time to clear the track before the 160 scheduled laps were completed.

As starter Harold Kinder waited with the yellow caution flag in hand, Petty and Yarborough sped around the track. Petty had the lead when Yarborough began to swing around him in the traditional slingshot that Petty discovered. Petty immediately swung back, remembering the early years when he would make his move too quickly.

"We touched two or three times," Petty said, "but not enough to upset either car."

At the finish line, Petty won by a foot, almost mimicking the way his father had won the inaugural Daytona 500 over Johnny Beauchamp 25 years earlier.

Yarborough was so flustered, he thought the race was over. He drove into the pits, then hurried back onto the track for the last lap and ended up third, with Harry Gant credited for second place.

• In 1985, Greg Sacks recorded what many considered the biggest upset in decades by edging Bill Elliott. Later, his crew chief confessed he may have "slipped" an oversized engine past inspectors.

• In 1987, Bobby Allison posted his 84th victory, but no one knew it at first. The scoreboard didn't record that Allison had managed to get back on the lead lap with nine laps to go, while Dave Marcis and Buddy Baker battled for the lead. A crash by Rick Wilson brought out a late caution flag with Marcis in the lead. Allison took advantage of the caution to pit for fresh tires, and came from 13th place to win—while the leaders assumed he was still a lap down.

• In 1988, Bill Elliott started in 38th, then edged Rick Wilson by three feet to win. "I had to radio the crew and have them tell me who won," Elliott said. "It was that close."

Nor is racing at the Speedway limited to NASCAR NEXTEL Cup. A NASCAR Busch Series event, which began as part of the Modified Sportsman division, is a regular fixture during Speedweeks, creating its own history. In 2002, a second NASCAR Busch Series races was added to the Pepsi 400 weekend.

"There's virtually no difference in the appearance of Winston Cup and Busch Series cars and certainly none in cost," according to Rick Houston, author of *Second to None: The History of the NASCAR Busch Series*. In the early years, the engines were not the same, but that changed in 2001 when NASCAR Busch Series cars began to use the identical 12-to-1 compression ratio as those of NASCAR NEXTEL Cup cars. The NASCAR Busch Series drivers tend to post slower speeds because of carburetor restrictions designed to help lower expenses.

Cost containment is why teams usually can change only three sets of tires under caution per race.

"Winston Cup cars weigh 3,400 pounds without their drivers, just 100 pounds more than those in the Busch Series," Houston continued. "The 105-inch wheelbase found in the Busch Series is five inches shorter than that of a Winston Cup car. Why the difference? Bigger cars, with wheelbases of up to 112 inches, were eligible for competition in the early years of the Busch Series. Older models were still in service in the mid-1980s. It wasn't uncommon to see cars that were seven and eight years old in competition.

"In an attempt to encourage Detroit manufacturers' involvement, NASCAR allowed shorter, current-year models in 1986 and mandated the 105-inch wheelbase, as well as the smaller V-6 engines that were then popular. Although V-8 engines returned in 1995, the 105-inch wheelbase remains unchanged."

The NASCAR Busch Series is now the second most-popular form of motorsports in this country, based on attendance figures. As with NASCAR NEXTEL Cup, some of the most unusual events in the NASCAR Busch Series have taken place in Daytona. They include:

• In 1959, when Banjo Matthews won the first Daytona race, then in the modified division, he declined to kiss Miss Speedway more than once, despite requests from photographers. He had promised his wife to limit himself to one.

• In 1960, there was a 37-car pile-up on the opening lap, causing a restart. There were still plenty of competitors—68 cars started the race.

SPEEDWEEKS

For two weeks in mid-February, Daytona Beach is more than the living embodiment of racing heritage. It becomes the complete focus of motorsports. At least 250,000 people pour into the small resort community to enjoy a parade of events featuring everything from sports cars to stock cars.

The array of races can be bewildering, even to serious fans of motorsports. Here's an introduction to the many races held during Speedweeks and a brief history of each series.

Rolex 24 At Daytona

This is the first race of the two-week extravaganza. Begun in 1966 as a three-hour event, the Rolex 24 At Daytona has expanded around the clock in the supreme test of man and machine. Cars compete in several classes and range from Daytona Prototype introduced in 2003 to the ultra-fancy Nissan Lola.

The participants in this Grand American Rolex Sports Car Series event are part of the Grand American Road Racing Association, which was founded in 2000 and sponsors timed events on tracks around the country. Drivers are world-renowned for their work in sports cars, and the series includes competitors drawn from NASCAR Winston Cup and other series.

There are other events during the Rolex 24 weekend. The schedule includes a race sponsored by:

• Grand-Am Cup. Once known as Motorola Cup, this race initiates a season on sports-car events also held at tracks around the country.

• Rolex Legends. This event displays vintage cars that have competed in previous Rolex 24 events.

• Historic race. Sponsored by the Historic Sportscar Racing Inc., this event features a variety of race cars that once competed in events. All are kept in excellent condition, and many sport their original colors.

Once the sports cars end their runs, the stock cars take over. There are five different stock-car series holding season openers during the two weeks. They are:

ARCA RE/MAX Series

The Automobile Racing Club of America (ARCA) was founded in 1953 in Toledo, Ohio as a Midwest-based, stock car auto racing sanctioning body. ARCA's founder, John Marcum, had raced against and worked as an official for Bill France, NASCAR's founder.

ARCA holds more than 100 race events each season in three professional touring series on a weekly basis. Some 400 race drivers are licensed by ARCA to compete for well over $3 million in prize monies each season.

The division of ARCA racing that is best known and that receives unquestionably the greatest amount of media exposure is the ARCA RE/MAX Series. This series has crowned an ARCA national champion each season since the inaugural season in 1953 and has toured more than 200 racetracks in 26 states since its inception. The ARCA RE/MAX Series is unusual in that it tests the abilities of drivers and race teams on perhaps the most diverse schedule of stock car racing events in the world. The series annually takes teams to tracks ranging in size from one-half mile to 2.66 miles in length, on both paved and dirt surfaces as well as left- and right-hand turn street and road courses.

The racecars are 3,400-pound, full steel-bodied stock cars, many of which originally were driven in the NASCAR NEXTEL Cup Series.

NASCAR Busch Series

Originally the Late Model Sportsman Division, the NASCAR Busch Series was created in 1982. Once simply a weekly series in the East, it became a national series considered one level below NASCAR Winston Cup. Drivers who are successful in the NASCAR Busch Series often find seats in NASCAR Winston Cup, but many drivers have chosen to carve out lucrative careers in this series.

The cars are virtually identical to NASCAR NEXTEL Cup cars, with a slight difference in horsepower. The drivers often compete on the same tracks and the same weekends as NASCAR NEXTEL Cup, which allows NASCAR NEXTEL

Cup drivers to enter Busch Series events. In 2001, for example, Kevin Harvick drove all Busch Series races—and won the championship—and missed only one NASCAR Winston Cup event. He was also Rookie of the Year in the NASCAR Winston Cup Series.

IPOWER Dash

In the 1950s, NASCAR started a separate division for its regional activities. At that time, one series was set up in the West, another in the East. Since then, booming interest in motor sports has helped the Touring Division expand into nine different units. The original western series is now Winston West. The eastern half evolved into several series, including the Featherlite Modified Series and the Busch North Series.

Only one of the nine touring series has competed at Daytona International Speedway—the *IPOWER* Dash Series, which races in the Southeastern part of the country.

The series serves as a training ground for young drivers or a less-expensive option for veterans looking to compete in late-model stock cars.

NASCAR sold the series in 2003 to BRDAYTONA, a Florida-based motorsports promotion company led by investors Randy Claypoole, former public relations director of the series, and Buck Parker.

International Race of Champions

An all-star event, IROC was created in 1974 to bring together 12 of the top race drivers in the world. They drive identical cars in a four-race series to determine who is the best. In 2003, the drivers competed at Daytona International Speedway, Indianapolis (Indiana) Motor Speedway, Chicagoland (Illinois) Speedway and Talladega (Alabama) Superspeedway.

The cars in recent years have been Pontiac Firebirds, and the drivers typically represent NASCAR Winston Cup, NASCAR Busch Series, the CART FedEx Championship Series and the Indy Racing League.

In the past 14 years, NASCAR Winston Cup drivers have dominated the championships. Kurt Busch won in 2003; Kevin Harvick in 2002.

NEXTEL Cup

Speedweeks concludes with the climactic running of the Daytona 500. The first race in the NASCAR NEXTEL Cup season, the Daytona 500 presents 43 of the top drivers in the world in a usually stirring and invariably tension-filled race into history.

NASCAR NEXTEL Cup is the current name for the elite series in NASCAR, which was founded in 1948. The drivers are drawn from various other series, such as the NASCAR Busch Series, the NASCAR Craftsman Truck Series and ARCA. They also may be plucked from the eight NASCAR touring series, such as West Series and Featherlite North.

In addition to the Daytona 500, NASCAR NEXTEL Cup drivers compete in two other events during Speedweeks:

• Qualifying. All drivers compete in normal qualifying with the front row set based on posted times.

• The Budweiser Shootout at Daytona. Once called the Bud Clash and the Bud Shootout, this event brings together pole winners from the previous year and former champions for a 70-lap sprint. The event is held the Sunday prior to the Daytona 500. At one time, drivers who were fastest during the second day of qualifying for any previous year's races competed in a 25-lap race, with the winner moving into the Budweiser Shootout. When second-day qualifying ended, so did the first race.

In 2000, the last year the qualifying race was held, Dale Jarrett won the qualifier and then the Budweiser Shootout, which then consisted of 25 laps. He was the only driver ever to complete that feat, but Jarrett added another star to his resume by taking the Daytona 500 that year, too.

• The Gatorade 125s. Two identical 50-lap events annually fill positions three through 43 in the grid for the Daytona 500. Originally, the races were 100 miles long, but they were increased to 125 in 1969. At one point, the late Dale Earnhardt won 10 Gatorade 125s in a row.

NASCAR Craftsman Truck Series

This is the only Speedweeks event not involving stock cars. The series began in 1996.

Ryan Newman's car was a battered hunk of metal when it finally came to rest during the 2003 Daytona 500. In a testament to the safety devices built into the car, he walked away unscathed and raced the following weekend.
Motorsports Images & Archives Photo

• In 1966, in his first race on the famed track after coming back from a suspension, Curtis Turner wore a rookie stripe on the rear of his car and recorded his 355th career win in all series inside and outside NASCAR.

• In 1967, Paul Goldsmith's crew took 33 seconds to change a tire and lost the race to Jim Paschal, who made up a huge deficit with a five-second stop for gas. Perhaps that's why Richard Petty once called Paschal, who won 25 NASCAR Winston Cup races, his favorite driver. The same race had back-to-back cautions caused by debris on the track—the caution flag fell off the pace car during the first caution.

Initially, NASCAR Busch Series events typically featured youngsters on their way to NASCAR Winston Cup or veterans either waiting a second chance or content to compete in shorter races. The schedule was often uneven, and no events were held west of the Mississippi River. All that changed quickly in the late 1990s as interest in motorsports continued to soar. The first western event took place in Las Vegas Motor Speedway in 1997.

In 2000 NASCAR Busch Series drivers competed in 32 races at 27 different tracks in 20 states, including California and Arizona. A year later, they made 34 stops in 22 different states.

Many competitors, enjoying the increased prestige and prize money, now do not hesitate to enjoy an entire career in the series. The best-known competitors include David Green, Stacy Compton and Mike McLaughlin. Many NASCAR NEXTEL Cup regulars also compete in selected NASCAR Busch Series events. Long-time NASCAR NEXTEL Cup star Mark Martin has posted more wins than anyone in the history of the NASCAR Busch Series.

In 2001, Kevin Harvick became the first driver to compete in almost a full NASCAR Winston Cup and Busch schedule. He only missed the Daytona 500. On several weekends, when races were held in different cities, he piled up frequent-flyer miles. In an incredible display of stamina, the Californian ended up winning the NASCAR Busch Series championship and finishing in the top 10 in NASCAR Winston Cup.

Daytona also added a third major NASCAR Series to its lineup in 2000. The NASCAR Craftsman Truck Series, begun in 1995, joined Speedweeks with a spectacular inaugural event that featured numerous mishaps. One fiery crash sent Geoffrey Bodine tumbling along the frontstretch. He escaped serious injury, but the accident caused officials to stop the race for more than two hours.

The second race at Daytona was especially exciting. Because a NASCAR Craftsman Truck Series race cannot end on a caution, the truckers had to line up for a two-lap sprint to the checkered flag. In front when the green flag waved for the single-file restart, Joe Ruttman, the oldest driver in any major NASCAR series, held his ground as Ricky Hendrick, son of current car-owner Rick Hendrick, and then Scott Riggs made charges at him.

"It was every man for himself," Hendrick said.

He wanted to wait until the last turn on the last lap to make a charge, but no drafting partners were close enough to help. Instead, Hendrick, who edged by Riggs on the final straightaway, could only watch helplessly as Ruttman posted his 12th career truck win.

"It appears to me that those young boys didn't look very far ahead," said Ruttman, who knows a lot about the long haul. "They got greedy. You need a partner here."

He had one—the trophy marking his first win at Daytona International Speedway since an ARCA race in 1982.

Like every other driver who has ever raced on this storied track, he knew exactly what his win meant. His comments in Victory Lane also encapsulated what Daytona has meant to everyone who has ever raced here.

"This is a really special track," said Ruttman, who had been chasing a Daytona victory for almost 20 years. "To win something here is thrilling beyond words."

Forty-three drivers compete in "The Great American Race" in 2003 with an appropriate symbol in the foreground. Motorsports Images & Archives Photo